In The Drink
Surviving the Alcoholic

Celeste Weingardt & Irene Henry

Copyright © 2018 Celeste Weingardt & Irene Henry

All rights reserved. Unauthorized reproduction,
in any manner, is prohibited.

Published by Seagull Publishing

ISBN: 978-0-9771465-0-5
Library of Congress Control Number: 2018940863

With apologies to Henry Wadsworth Longfellow

There was a little missy,
who got a little tipsy,
And could not get her life sorted.

When she was sober,
she was likable indeed,
But when she was drunk she was horrid.

CONTENTS

Introduction 1

Our Stories

Siblings of Alcoholics. *Our brothers and sisters* 3
Gone Too Soon 5
Prayers and Best Intentions 9
The Long Reach of Family 21
Misplaying a Bad Hand 27
Waiting for the Inevitable 33

Spouses of Alcoholics. *Married to an alcoholic* 39
Drinking Buddies 41
A Selfish Man 45
I Choose 51
Making Good on Second Chances 55
Hidden Bottles 61

Children of Alcoholics. *Growing up with a drinking parent* 67
Like Father, Like Son 69
Boots 81
The Patriarch 87
The Illusion of a Privileged Life 91

Parents of Alcoholics. *The heartbreak of being the parent of an alcoholic.* 99
Identity Crossroads 101
Lost at 40 107
Dry Drunk 111

A Way Forward

Your Wellbeing is Our Primary Concern 117
Navigating the Traps 121
What Success Stories Have In Common 127
Taking Control 131
Final Thoughts 135

Resources 137
Acknowledgements 139
About the Authors 140

INTRODUCTION

If you picked up this book, chances are you have a personal connection to someone with a drinking problem and are looking for answers. Excessive, out-of-control drinking blazes a wide path of devastation. The addiction not only consumes the drinker, but also wreaks havoc in the lives of those closest to them.

Alcoholism is often kept hidden as an embarrassing, somehow shameful family secret. This was our experience. We accidentally learned that we each had a brother suffering from alcoholism when they were both diagnosed with cancer around the same time, a concern that we *were* able to share with each other. Little by little, their life stories came out and we found that giving voice to our closely guarded family skeleton was a huge release. There was a measure of healing in the act of simply letting the secret out. Knowing first-hand how difficult it is to reach out, we are sharing our stories, and the stories of others, here. Through honest examination of these experiences, we hope to offer insight and perspective into how alcoholism manifests in a family.

In Part I of this book, we share our own stories and also the personal accounts of others who have problem drinkers in their own families. The stories that friends related to us are heart breaking and hopeful, discouraging and redemptive. Some take us to dark places. A few are narratives of possibilities resurrected. Others tell of individuals who made valiant efforts – whether successful or not – to overcome their addictions. We are forever grateful to our brave friends who shared their personal stories.

This book is based on real people and experiences, to the extent that these stories are the product of imperfect memories. Some details have been obscured and names changed out of consideration to extended family members whose privacy we wish to protect. We believe we have stayed true to the emotions, the tone of interactions and the essence of the individual dramas.

As the perspective and impact on family members vary significantly based on the familial connection, we have organized the stories by relationships: Siblings, Spouses, Parents and Children of alcoholics.

Following each narrative, we offer our thoughts on how the narrator's life was impacted by the alcoholic's behavior and how they dealt with it. Were they able to be a helpful influence to the alcoholic in any way? What steps did they take for self-protection?

In Part II, we summarize in general terms what we have learned about how alcoholism affects families. We look at factors consistent in the recovering alcoholic's lives and in the lives of those who remain trapped. Through better understanding of the underlying dynamics that contribute to addiction, we hope to arm others with information to help navigate a relationship with the alcoholic and assert more power over their own lives. As we are reminded in the Serenity Prayer, we can only change things within our control and must find the wisdom to let go of things we cannot change.

We conclude with a short list of resources and suggested reading. There are numerous published academic and scientific studies, books, and papers on alcoholism. There are support groups like Al-Anon.

We do not pretend to be experts in the field of alcoholism. What we do bring are our first hand observations and understanding coupled with a sincere desire to help others in the same position. We hope that you will gain some clarity and direction in your personal situation from reading these pages. We wish you peace.

Celeste and Irene

Siblings
our brothers and sisters

Growing up within the intimate confines of a private household, siblings share the good times and the bad, the family quirks and, sadly, sometimes dark family secrets. A sibling can be your best friend or the one who knows too well how to push your buttons. Sometimes they can be both. If there was addiction, trauma or abuse in the household, survivor's guilt can develop if one sibling breaks free of that negative cycle but their sibling does not.

Have you attempted to have a heart-to-heart with your sibling about their drinking? If this is something you want to do, go for it. Before you have the conversation, though, be clear on what, if any, support you are willing to offer and under what conditions.

Start by presenting the facts as you see them. Be calm and allow for a two-way conversation. If you smell BS, say so, but avoid a confrontational or accusatory tone. If you speak from a place of sincerity, they will hear you. What they do with that information is up to them, however. And when you're satisfied that you've done your best, it's time to move on.

GONE TOO SOON
Mary's Story

How can a drinking problem escalate from a few found empty bottles to death in so short a time? A family is left with broken hearts and questions that will forever remain unanswered when a young man tragically dies of liver failure from excessive drinking.

We had a middle-class suburban upbringing. Dad was a Ventura County Sheriff. Mom started an at-home licensed childcare business called "Rompers." Most of the kids that came to the daycare lived in our neighborhood, were our friends. We went to the same elementary school through high school, trick-and-treated together, toilet-papered houses and played pony league baseball. One of my most cherished sibling pictures is where we are each wearing our favorite team's uniform. Loren in his Mariner's uniform, Tyler in his Cub's uniform and myself a Dodger, the photo shot as we were walking side by side, arms touching arms.

My parents were OK with both of my brothers attending the local public high school in Port Hueneme. For me however, I got to go to Villanova Preparatory in Ojai. My high school games of choice were basketball, softball and volleyball. For Tyler it was football, and Loren played both high school basketball and volleyball. My Dad and siblings were very supportive in attending each other's high school games whenever possible. Not so much Mom 'cause she had the at-home child care business and then had to switch gears to get dinner ready and the household chores of the day complete.

Loren became the Villanova Volleyball coach my senior year and Dad became the bus driver for the Villanova away games. For our home games, Dad sometimes served as scorekeeper and was known around campus as 'Papa Wiggins.' When we were playing the away games, Papa Wiggins would sit on the highest bleacher, back to the wall and, with his deep voice, would bellow out the alleged mistake; "Come on Nova…What was that?" or cheer "good shot."

Loren's drinking wasn't brought to light until after I graduated from Syracuse and returned home from college in 2010. He would come home with a brown paper bag or a bulge under his coat and disappear into his bedroom. We later discovered Loren was going to his bedroom to drink Jack Daniels.

In 2011, in his first attempt at detoxing, Loren tried to do it on his own. I'm unsure how long he stuck with it. Days, weeks? Loren had been at home, restless, and went out for a walk one evening. A policeman found him at 2:00 a.m., collapsed on the sidewalk. Loren ended up in the hospital for 14 days. The doctor told us that Loren's system was weak; his liver's enzyme levels were that of a 60-year-old who had been drinking all his life rather than that of a 30-year-old. They were not sure his body would recover. Loren was given a prescription of Ativan to help with sleep and to not be so agitated.

A few months later, while coaching a volleyball practice at Villanova high school, Loren had a seizure and was admitted to Ojai Community Hospital. He was released 10 days later. Even knowing that he had a compromised liver and that he needed to stop drinking, he still resisted the idea of going into a rehab program. But he did try AA for a short time after the hospitalization.

The summer of 2013, our brother Tyler, his wife Amy and their son Roland moved to Arizona. Loren was coaching at a Club volleyball tournament in Phoenix and I had to be in town at the same time. We were all getting together for a BBQ at Tyler's. Loren seemed a bit off. The big tell was when Loren said he was taking off for an errand, which would have made him gone for quite some time and instead he returned in such a short time that we knew the "errand " could not possibly have occurred. We went to his car and found empty bottles of alcohol and knew right then we needed to say something to Loren about his drinking.

Loren was in the backyard checking out the burgers and ribs on the BBQ. Amy was playing with Roland in the pool. Tyler and I both went into the backyard. Tyler took his six-foot-three-inches, 219 lbs. and positioned himself directly in front of his older brother, dwarfing Loren's five-feet-eleven-inches, 165 lbs. and called Loren out on his lying, his drinking. Amy took Roland out of the pool and went into their home, as my brothers yelled at each other. Their heated argument resulted in Loren walking out.

After Arizona, Tyler said that Roland was not to be in a car with Loren while he was in this drinking mode. Amy, my sister-in-law, judgment-free and from a place of pure love and caring, offered to go with Loren to AA or wherever he wanted or needed to be to get to a better place. Not once did Loren take Amy up on her offer. Around this same time, I started to notice that when Loren needed a drink his hands would shake and he would be short-tempered.

My family is close; we talk, though we do not really communicate about deep issues. (The sex talk did not come from my mom rather from my older girl cousins, though not discussing sex with her only daughter could have been more about the subject matter and Mom's generation.)

The family conversation regarding Loren's drinking was no different. The family, minus Loren, had a conversation with the doctor at Ojai Community Hospital. At this meeting the picture my parents painted for the doctor was one of Loren as an occasional drinker. Tyler and I had to inform the doctor what we found in his bedroom: full and empty bottles of hard liquor with receipts in the trash indicating the Jim Beam was purchased and emptied the same day. We explained to our parents that this was "serious" drinking. Our parents needed a reality check. Loren was indeed an alcoholic.

There was not a particular "polaroid moment" catapulting Loren to his drinking that I know of. I think Loren felt this weight as the older brother that it was his responsibility to lead the way, set the example for his younger siblings to be successful in life, and he felt he failed.

Since graduating with a Masters in Film and Art from Brooks Institute, Loren had been working on scripts with a group down in the LA area. Nothing was happening — maybe there were a lot of script rejections. I was a Syracuse University graduate, now working towards my Master's Degree in Depth Psychology and was working full-time in a group transitional home. Our younger brother Tyler was happily married to Amy, both gainfully employed. Their son Roland made them the perfect family. Loren's success would have been defined for himself in having one of his many screenplays produced or to have an occupation in that line of work.

In January 2015, Loren made his third attempt at self-detox. He collapsed again and was admitted to Community Memorial Hospital for two days. Loren took Ativan that evening for sleep. We believe Loren's system was too beaten, too taxed. When he went to sleep he did not have enough left in him to wake up to one more sunrise.

If it were possible to go back and do something differently, maybe I would have talked with Loren more about his drinking. Maybe. We had one serious heart to heart where I told him it was not right for me "to bury my older brother." However, one has to remember this is not the kind of family that I was raised in; we did not really talk about substantive issues.

Though, while Loren was alive and living in their home after his hospitalization, my parents removed all the alcohol from the house, even after Loren's death, I sincerely believe my mom believes Loren was not an alcoholic.

My worst nightmare came true when I buried my older brother. Loren, you used to say to me when I missed a pitch or hit a serve in the net or skinned a knee, "Walk it off." This I cannot "walk off" and it will not make it any easier because I will be missing you, always.

Our Thoughts

Mary was only in her early 20's when Loren's alcoholism became an obvious problem, causing her to have to radically reconsider a big brother whom she had looked up to. His drinking caused a lot of tension in the family, which had once been very close. Loren's brother was confrontational about the drinking. The parents were in denial. The sister-in-law tried to gently persuade Loren to get help and offered to stand by him, an offer he declined.

The entire family wishes they had seen the signs of Loren's drinking sooner. He had a deficient liver that the excessive drinking caused to deteriorate far more rapidly than would have occurred otherwise. Because no one had really talked to Loren about the drinking, they were only able to second-guess what caused him to drink so heavily. Mary is left with many unanswered questions and a lot of regrets. She wishes that her parents had acted on her and her brother Tyler's concerns when they found the empty bottles.

The family reacted in two extremes: the parents in denial, the brother confrontational. Neither is an effective approach. Mary and the sister-in-law had better approaches, but not enough time.

PRAYERS AND BEST INTENTIONS
Celeste's Story

Celeste and her brother started drinking in their early teens. Their drinking became pronounced enough by early adulthood that each stood to lose their spouses. Both put forth a sincere effort to stop drinking and yet only one was able to break free of the power that alcohol held over them. Here is their story.

It was the summer I was 12 years old and my brother Larry was 14. The long days loomed endlessly before us. It would be weeks before we had to start thinking about the coming school year.

We were hanging out under the Gully Bridge with a handful of other kids. Two of the older boys had rigged up a rope swing from the bridge. At the top of the slope where the sandy, hard packed earth was only a couple of feet below the length of heavy rope, several kids held the line steady while another kid straddled the large knot at its end. Once they let go, the rider swung out over the expanse of gully and then back up the slope. Hopefully, the momentum was right and the kids on the ground were able to catch the rope on the upswing enabling an easy dismount. Otherwise, the rider needed to jump before it started on the downward trajectory again, necessitating a drop into uneven ground covered with blackberry brambles.

The swing was definitely intimidating. One of the older guys teased Larry about being afraid to go on it. He goaded Larry all afternoon. After chugging a beer Larry started working up his nerve. By the time he finished a second, he was swaggering, ready for his turn.

No one accounted for the weight difference between Larry and the older boys when they gave him the push off. We all held our breath when he flew across the gully, swinging farther out than any of the others had and rising up, almost touching the bridge's cross supports on the opposite side before swinging back to us. His drop, tuck and roll was not pretty. Everybody had another beer after that.

Happily, Larry didn't sustain substantial injuries that day. I'd like to say that we both learned a valuable lesson that summer about risk-taking, about muddled thinking when we'd been drinking, or at least about being pushed into doing something against our better judgment. But some things we did not learn easily.

The Neighborhood Bar

We lived in a solidly middle-class bedroom community with manicured front lawns and trimmed hedges. Most dads were white-collar workers. Many of the moms were homemakers. There were a few upmarket apartment buildings along the main boulevard. The bar was within walking distance amid a cluster of fast food restaurants, a liquor store and a professional building with real estate, law and accounting offices.

I don't recall the bar's name. I always just thought of it as "The Bar." Every neighborhood has one. They are dark and scuffed. Its heart is a pool table. The regulars know each other by name. Sometimes that's all they know about each other. Even after years of bending elbows together on a nightly basis, conversation revolved around sports, cars and the weather.

At fifteen I used to dread walking that stretch of the boulevard. The whistles and catcalls were new to me and frightening. At seventeen I was a weekend semi-regular at The Bar.

My brother infiltrated it first. No one asked his age or mine. We didn't bring friends there until we were familiar to all the bartenders. Too many underage patrons would bring unwanted attention to us.

There was a single room about the size of an overlarge living room. The bar was in the back. Drinkers faced themselves in the veined and cloudy mirror mounted behind the clutter of bottles. The pool table's green felt was dulled with age, spilled beer and cigarette ash. It was easily older than I was. On a busy night, it, along with the foosball table, pinball machine and jukebox were in constant use.

My strongest memories of the bar are odor related. Stale beer, stale cigarettes. If the bathrooms were cleaned on a regular basis, it was not apparent by look or smell. Wet floor. Strewn paper towels. Overflowing toilet. Urine with an under note of vomit. I was told that the men's room was worse. The lighting, even during the day, was faint. No wall hangings or decoration. This was no *Cheers* set.

It did have its redeeming graces, though. This wasn't a pick-up place. If a guy occasionally bothered me, one of the regulars would intervene, and fighting would get a person banned for life. I rarely had to pay for my drinks. What adrift seventeen year-old could ask for more?

Larry was nineteen and still chipping away at a handful of classes that he needed in order to get his high school diploma. He was working full time as a gas station attendant. He had a cool little 'bachelor pad', his term. It was a small apartment above the garage of one of the grander homes by the park. A spiral wrought iron staircase, wall-to-wall shag carpet and an orange freestanding ceramic fireplace were its standout features. It became the go-to place for us all to hang out for a time. We'd play oldies on the stereo, and, of course, drink beer.

One evening four of us decided to head down to the bar to play some pool. We piled into the car and drove the ten or so blocks down the hill. It was a Friday night and the place was packed. Larry and one of his friends muscled through the crowd and got us a couple of pitchers. And then we had a few more.

By closing time, none of us were seeing straight and yet we all jumped back in the car with Larry behind the wheel. Thank goodness Gus came out after us. He was gorgeous, super nice and had an awesome car. I usually drank a lot less when I thought there was a chance he would be coming in. The glimpse of me that I saw through his eyes that night was unsettling. I wasn't drunk enough to miss his disapproving look as he arranged for a friend to follow us in his car and then drove us all home.

Through our teen years I had other moments of recognition that the two of us drank more excessively that most of our peers. For myself, there were a few nasty hangovers and morning regrets that caused me to temper my behavior, at least for a period. I don't remember Larry ever experiencing hangovers, though, even though he drank copious amounts of beer. He wasn't one to slur his words or stumble. Larry liked to boast that he could drink anyone under the table and chided his drinking buddies for pacing their consumption. "Lightweight" was a favorite derision of his. He would sometimes get boisterous and macho in his behavior as the night progressed —typical guy posturing stuff. The more he drank, the more he bragged.

I started working at an insurance company in downtown L.A. right out of high school, moved out of the house and gravitated to a new group of friends. I was anxious to start a new life in the adult world and separate myself from some poor choices and embarrassing memories. My brother and I drifted apart. There was no rift between us, just moving in different directions. I relocated up the coast when I was 21 and saw little of my brother for the next couple of years.

About the same time that I moved north, Larry got a job as a cabinetmaker. It was a pretty decent income and the job had potential. One day a nail gun misfired, blinding him in one eye. He was unable to go back to cabinet making after he healed as it was not safe for him to use the tools with his compromised sight. I had never seen him truly depressed before. Something changed in Larry after the accident. It seemed as though he lost a lot of his drive. His drinking persona became morose and reflective at times.

The following decade was devoted to both Larry and myself starting families of our own. My husband's job eventually brought us back to Southern California when our son was in second grade and our daughter was two years old. My brother got married and he and his wife had four kids. The kids loved having cousins, and the extended family shared holidays and many birthdays at our parents' house. My brother and I were always happy to see each other, but never rekindled the level of closeness we had shared growing up.

My Story

I was the kind of alcoholic who found it extremely hard to stop drinking once I got going. My social skills were tied to my drinking, too; when I didn't drink I felt awkward, unattractive, and uninteresting. A drink or two would boost my self-confidence and lessen my severe inhibitions. (I haven't danced since my last drink.)

I continued to drink throughout my twenties and early thirties but did so mostly at home, on my own. We didn't go out much, but when we did I would fortify myself with several drinks before we left the house. Embarrassment or regret sometimes motivated me to put the bottle away for a day or even a week. I made private bargains with myself. But inevitably I drank again. I did most of my living inside my head. I could be successful in my daydreams, but if I took real action, I could fail. I didn't talk to anyone about my fears or struggles.

There were a few harsh should-have-been wake up calls along the way. One time my husband and I were on vacation, having a great time. We treated ourselves to an extravagant steak and lobster dinner at a four-star restaurant. There were cocktails before dinner, wine with the meal and after dinner drinks. And then I kept drinking well past the time I should have stopped. With my normal filters drowned in vodka, Chablis and brandy, bottled up frustrations and complaints came spewing out of my mouth. Words that hurt, charges that were at best half-truths and issues that were under my control, not his. If there had been a flight available for him to leave that night instead of being forced to stay in the city with me where we had the opportunity to talk things out in the light of a new day, our marriage might well have ended then.

I finally got myself to Alcoholics Anonymous. I was one of the lucky ones. I found a group that I felt comfortable with right away. All women, many with stories similar to my own. I did not suffer an intense daily struggle to resist drinking as many recovering alcoholics do. I was not around a lot of drinking situations that tested me in those critical early months. I had a husband who encouraged me to go to as many meetings as I felt I needed even though he had to take on a larger share of parenting responsibilities.

I was given support, understanding, and importantly, tools and tips to cope. Like having a glass of club soda in hand at all times during parties so that others wouldn't press drinks on me, learning what triggers set me off, picking up the phone before picking up the glass. The AA clichés have seen me through many a challenging moment: progress, not perfection; act as if and the rest will follow; get out of self; and the most famous one, One Day at a Time. Lifesavers all.

I started drinking at such an early age that it was incredibly scary to face the world without alcohol to prop me up. Losing the shield that drinking provided meant, to me, having to meet the world without armor. Learning to interact with others felt like having to create a personality from scratch. But with newly acquired life skills and, admittedly, a good dose of luck, I connected with new interests and developed a community of acquaintances whom I aspired to be like. I began to fill the void that loomed large in my life when I quit drinking, replacing negative habits with positive ones.

Another Round in Rehab

For the next several years while I was learning to live without alcohol, Larry's life took a sharp downhill turn. Binge drinking led to multiple blackout episodes. He couldn't hold a job. He told me that he and his wife constantly fought. Ultimately, he left the house and joined the ranks of the homeless. He was so focused on his inner demons and his obsession with alcohol that even his love for his wife and family couldn't pull him out of his self-destructive spiral.

His communication with the extended family became nearly nonexistent. He cut himself off almost completely from our parents, and my sister and I only heard from him when he needed money. The Ask was always preceded by some long, involved tale of woe. Someone or something external had caused whatever crisis was at hand. I wanted to shout at him to just get to it and stop insulting my intelligence with his transparent attempts at emotional manipulation. We often gave him money in the end, though. For love or guilt.

I hadn't spoken to Larry in nine months when I received a terse call from a rehab center administrator. Larry had designated me his emergency contact. He guessed correctly that I would come, even though he knew that Mom, Sis and I had promised each other that we wouldn't get sucked into his drama again. Part of my mission was to make him understand that I wouldn't do this again. Really.

The rehab center was located on a quiet, tree-lined street sandwiched between modest professional offices. At the other end of the block there was a row of apartment buildings with sheets in the windows and lawns that needed watering.

The privately run facility offered the standard 30-day program. Medi-Cal was picking up the tab. The walls in the visitor's room were institutional green. There were no windows. The floor was aging linoleum. He was sitting, slumped, at a bare, utilitarian table, the only person in the room. I immediately wanted to leave.

I was hesitant to hug him. He seemed fragile in both body and mind. Larry had always been thin but that day he looked emaciated. He'd been living in homeless shelters when he was sober and on the streets when he wasn't. Mostly, he'd been on the streets. This hard existence was taking its toll and it showed.

I was on the brink of tears, barely holding it together. I handed over the plastic grocery bag with the cigarettes, toothbrush and paste, soap, Dr. Pepper and chocolate pudding cups he had requested. Then I handed him the Burger King bag, which he wasn't expecting. A Whopper, fries and chocolate shake may not be high on the nutrition scale, but I hoped that it would pique his appetite. The administrator had told me that he wasn't eating and that felt like a small way in which I might actually help.

The conversation was difficult. As far as I knew, Larry had stayed sober for more than a year after the last trip to rehab. He had seemed to be doing ok. He had answered my weekly calls. And then my calls started going direct to voicemail. And then the number was no longer in service. And then no word until the call from rehab.

I braced myself and asked how he was feeling. I was tiptoeing, not knowing what might cause either of us to break down. I was mad at him for doing this to himself. To the family. But I didn't want to hurt him. I knew he was hurting plenty already. He was hunched into himself and wouldn't make eye contact. I was glad that he has the meal to focus on, to fiddle with. The distraction made this bearable.

For twenty painful minutes we talked. Nothing probing or critical. I didn't ask where he'd been for these last months or how he found his way to this rehab center. I figured he would tell me when he was ready. I left with a promise to come again in two days. He asked me to call his kids and let them know that he loved them.

After thirty days, Larry was released from rehab. He was anxious to put this horrible episode behind him. The DT's were bad, bad, bad, but they nursed him through it. He had regained a measure of health. He had even put on a few pounds. They armed him with leads for employment and set him up with temporary housing.

Larry leaned heavily on his church. He attended bible classes and received counseling from the pastor. He tried AA once but didn't like the people or structure. He told me that he was certain that Jesus would see him through his struggles and fend off his demons. He just needed to pray harder. This was a touchy subject between us. My impulse was to share 12-step advice that had resonated for me. He tended to shut down at the mere mention of AA. I likened his attitude to that of a person who treats his pneumonia with herbal supplements instead of prescription medication. Why not use every means available to foster a good outcome?

The next couple of years were rocky. He came to family get-togethers. He was sober and fun and glad to be with us. He would be quick to help with kitchen duties and entertaining the kids. He won and lost at cards graciously. He chatted easily with his brothers-in-law.

But he was frustrated with dead end jobs and complained to me that others didn't recognize his ability or worth. He began drinking once again. Eventually his wife asked for a divorce.

Certain that a fresh start would fix all of his problems, Larry moved a few towns north, close to where one of our sisters lived. He stopped drinking. New beginnings. Everything would be different, better. He gambled that enough time had passed since the last time he ensnared our sister in his drama that he would be welcomed into her life again. She was skeptical at first and kept Larry at arms length, but he attended church with her regularly and quietly settled in.

He had his makeover life, his New Beginning, and two sisters now back in his life. Checking in. Lending him moral support … and dollars. His life revolved around his new church — in particular, its food pantry. Larry proved himself a valuable asset to the program and was soon managing it; ordering supplies, organizing volunteers, even cooking. He enjoyed the appreciation of the church community. If only this could have become his paid employment.

The church always managed to come through with something, but it was job-by-job, minimum pay. My suggestion that he could use his experience running the food pantry to find a job in a commercial kitchen fell on deaf ears. Fear of rejection? Fear of stepping out of the protective church environment? If only I could have convinced him to try. If only he had given it a shot. His self-esteem, self-image was in dire need of a boost.

For several months, he shared a house with a young guy who worked for a high performance auto shop. He hooked Larry up with some hours at the shop, too. The shop owner was "a little short" one week and again the next. Larry never got paid. He resumed doing odd jobs for church members and contracted to paint a fixer-upper that a young couple had recently purchased. After that, trying to find something less physically taxing, he took on a route for a church member who had a vending machine business, restocking the machines. Our sister lent him a new truck so that he would have reliable transportation for the early morning, seventy-mile loop. Larry was truly excited about what he characterized as a business opportunity. He was making lofty plans for the fortune soon to come. Putting his kids through college. Paying off his ex-wife's mortgage. He lived this delusion for several months before the reality of his actual, limited financial prospects sank in. He was hurt that someone he trusted has used him. No point in mentioning a lifelong pattern of being drawn into schemes that didn't paid off, at least for him.

The weight of poor health and depression

Chaucer wrote, "All good things must come to an end," to which an unattributed line has been added: "But all bad things can continue forever." How depressing. And for my brother, perhaps too true.

Larry would answer my phone calls, but begged off visits more often than not. His physical health was visibly worsening. He had worn a beard for years, an ineffective attempt to draw attention away from his bad teeth. When he showed up at his youngest daughter's high school graduation, the beard was long and unkempt. He was bundled up in a quilted parka in spite of the fact that it was a warm June evening. After the ceremony, he posed for photos, smiling and embracing his daughter, but was uncharacteristically quiet and gave excuses not to join the rest of us for dinner.

How had no one noticed the decline until now? How had an entire season passed since I last saw him?

Shortly after the graduation, a young couple from the church invited Larry to live with them. They lived miles from their nearest neighbors on a sparsely populated windy, two lane road that ran through a national forest. It would be reassuring to them for a good, Christian man to be around the house during the four-day stretches when the husband was at work at the fire station. And they had big plans to open a second hand store in a town at the edge of the high desert. Larry could help them get the storefront that they had leased ready for business. He would be a partner in the enterprise. A handshake contract.

Larry was bursting with enthusiasm and making plans. He watched their daughter and did chores around the house while the husband and wife worked on the store. Or he worked on the store on his own. On weekends they made the rounds of swap meets and garage sales to buy starter inventory. Since Larry was getting room and board and the promise of future profits, they weren't paying him for his work.

With the dollar outlay for the store lease and the inventory purchases, money soon became tight. The husband and wife were both becoming short tempered with Larry, with their child, with each other.

Larry hardly ever called me anymore, so at first I was happy to hear from him when he called out of the blue one day. He spoke in circles; the way people do when they have something on their mind but don't know how to say it. He told me about his back hurting and that the firefighter had him hanging upside down on some sort of contraption to realign his spine. So, maybe not drunk as I first suspected, but in the kind of pain that makes one incoherent. Whatever the possible merits of this type of therapy, it was clearly the wrong Rx for my brother's condition.

When I advised a consultation with an actual doctor, he was full of excuses for why it wasn't feasible. He would have to drive all the way down to Northridge to access the county health system and he could not drive himself that distance. He would have to spend all day waiting to be seen and the wife needed him to help at the house. Plus, no gas money. My proposal to pick him up was deflected. My offer to come by to see him was somehow never answered. He became agitated by my questions and ended the call abruptly, in the way a sullen teenager shuts down.

The next call, several days later, was collect from a pay phone in Lancaster. He seemed artificially upbeat. He rambled and made little sense. I had a nagging feeling that he probably had been drinking. As much as I had misgivings with his reliance on the church, I proposed that he visit his pastor, hoping that he could feel out the situation better than I and provide some counseling before things got worse. Whether it was drinking or health issues, something was clearly wrong. He was non-committal and the call ended unsatisfactorily for both of us. I tried calling his cell phone a week later, but a recording said it was out of service.

After another two-month gap in communication, he promised to be at Thanksgiving with the extended family, but then called to cancel. He said he fell and hurt his back so needed to take it easy for a few days.

Two days after Thanksgiving, my sister sent a lengthy email to me and our other sisters. A church elder had informed her that our brother was drinking again. She was clearly frustrated. More than any of the rest of us, she and her husband had been coming to Larry's rescue financially for many years. Additionally, she was feeling both guilty and embarrassed for having brought him into her church community.

The church, as a final act of charity, recommended that Larry be sent to a local Christian rehabilitation center. He had no money, no place to live. He had a dislocated shoulder and two broken ribs due to a recent fall. My sister lobbied for a united front. No money. No other assistance unless he entered this rehab program. Tough love. She had already spoken to our mother and gotten her agreement.

By the first week of December – the day before his 58th birthday, we received word that he had entered the program. I was encouraged that the program included a 12-step component rather than relying solely on spiritual guidance.

Our sister who was close to the church provided periodic updates from the pastor but with little detail. In part exhaustion from the many years of stressing over Larry and in part to keep a safe distance in an effort to maintain the united front of tough love that my mom, sisters and I had agreed to, I did not call or visit Larry myself. Months passed and my concerns for my brother receded. I sent a few thinking-of-you cards, but mostly he was out of sight and out of mind.

In late July, the church notified our sister that Larry was in the hospital. He had been in the hospital for three weeks but had only that day given them authority to contact us. He had initially been diagnosed with pneumonia but a subsequent MRI showed a mass. Cancer.

Although we had been told that the cancer was too far advanced to be treated, he seemed to be feeling better than we had anticipated. I wasn't aware at this point that the physician had also prescribed anti-anxiety medication.

At one point we had Mom, Larry's two daughters, my daughter, one brother-in-law and all of us sisters jammed into his hospital room. His oldest daughter donned a surgical mask and gloves and played the clown and had us all hooting with laughter. We had a nurse take a photo of us crowded around Larry's bed.

One of the sisters made a deli run and we all picnicked in his room, sharing chairs and making use of every flat surface to perch cups of coke and ice tea. It was healing for all parties to have these precious moments together. Larry's children told me that they and their mom would all do their best to be supportive and help give him peace and closure. I knew how much it meant to him to have them there and to receive, if not forgiveness, compassion. This is the image I hold in my memory of those last days.

We were touched that a good number of the church folks as well as extended family came to the funeral. The large sanctuary was more than half full by the time the service began. His son spoke warmly and elegantly about him and displayed an understanding of the struggles and demons that his father battled throughout his life. Our sister compiled written memories from family members that the pastor read during the service. Silly stories about running around the neighborhood in our pajamas and catching fireflies on hot summer nights, skateboarding in the basement, playing with the cousins at our grandparents house. Good times, when we were still young and innocent. Funerals are for the living, to bring us comfort and closure, but I think Larry would have been touched by the way in which we remembered him and I hope that, however this universe works, he felt the love we sent his way.

Many of us in the immediate family have struggled with second-guessing whether we could have done more for him. Ultimately I hold on to the belief that nothing I could have done differently, really at any stage, would have influenced a better outcome. His was a hard life and whether that was of his own making or not is now beside the point. Rest in peace, brother.

Our Thoughts

While it had been obvious for years that Larry had a severe drinking problem, the siblings didn't get directly involved until he had essentially lost everything. They frequently kept their distance even then because they often felt used and manipulated. On the many occasions when he came to them for money, they had to deal with either the stress on their own finances created by helping him out or with the stress that came from saying no, always fearing what might come next – worrying that he was so fragile that any little setback could break him. They were also weighed down by keeping secrets from other family members: not telling their parents what was going on in an effort to shield them; not telling the other sisters for fear they would be criticized for how they were handling things. There was also a great deal of resentment at being caught up in his problems, so much of the assistance they did lend came with a gray shadow of hostility.

The sisters cycled through a gamut of approaches. When Larry appeared to be making an effort they tried to stay in close touch, reaching out to him with regular phone calls, giving him money. When he didn't seem to be making an effort to get his life in order, or several times when they felt taken advantage of, they distanced themselves. And at times when things seemed to be going OK or they had their own issues to focus on, they gave little thought to Larry until the next holiday or the next crisis. In between the close times and the estrangements, one sister encouraged him to get involved with AA, and when he resisted, tried to share parts of AA practices that she hoped would resonate. His other sister would often go to church with him.

It would have helped if the family had been more candid with one another. If they had compared notes, they would have discovered that he had been tapping each of them for money over the years and convincing them not to mention it to the rest of the family, so they were unaware of the cumulative amount of support he was getting. They would have had not only a clearer picture of his circumstances, but could have gained emotional support from one another and the benefit of talking through decisions with someone else, and not have secrets as a barrier between them. Toward the end, they did finally made a group decision to not give any more help unless he went into a recovery program.

Larry, to a great degree, fits the profile of a dry drunk: extended periods without drinking, but not addressing personality traits or behavior to better deal with the world. The family's efforts to support him through the years, to reinforce the fact that he was a valued member of the family, probably helped him sustain several long stretches of sobriety. The narrator and others made an effort to be respectful of his dependence on religion and the church community; suggesting other assistance more directly related to alcoholism that would be of benefit to him, but not pressing him as that would likely have alienated him. The family is better off emotionally in dealing with Larry's death because they provided as much support over the years as they did. And they finally found support from one another.

THE LONG REACH OF FAMILY
Teresa's Story

Lost at the tail end of a large family, one sister is alienated from the family for many years, then finds her way to sobriety with the help of a good man, a caring community and a family that finally understands her secret history.

I am part of a large German/Scottish family with ten children. My mother had been married before and had two children. Her first husband was a philanderer who slept with everybody in town. She left him; packed up the kids and moved across the country to live with my grandmother in Los Angeles.

My mother got a job at a large insurance company where she met her second husband, my father. When he was in high school, in a seminary, he contracted a bone infection that severely damaged his hip. This was in the days before penicillin. Because of this, he had one leg that was shorter than the other. Unlike many of his peers, he was not able to serve in the military during WWII. His job was to drive the cars of servicemen to where they were stationed so that they had their cars.

When my parents got married, he took in her two children, my half-siblings, and then they had eight more kids. I was number eight. We were young kids when our older brothers and sisters were moving out of the house and starting their own families — there was 20 years between the oldest and the youngest. Still, I always felt that we were a close family. We went to church every Sunday and spent a lot of time with my dad's brothers and sisters.

We had a lot of fun. The adults drank but there was never anyone I remember as being out of control. As our family grew older with more adults, we would socialize more with alcohol around. Have wine. Go out for Mexican food and have margaritas.

My youngest sister, Barb, being the baby, was a little bit left out. The rest of us were in high school when she was in grammar school. By the time she got to high school we had graduated. So maybe it was more like there were two clusters of siblings and then there was Barb. She was always trying to catch up with us, wanting to please us. We thought she was being a little pest. But we would have to take her with us. This wasn't an unusual situation in large families, but my sister took it very personally. It festered with her, that feeling of isolation. She didn't feel like she belonged, but she idolized us at the same time.

When she got to high school, Barb had a lot of friends. She was good looking. I know now, many years after the fact, that she was raped while on a date when she was in high school. She didn't share that with anybody at the time. She kept it inside because she was humiliated. And she thought no one would believe her. Her behavior changed. She flirted openly with our boyfriends, our husbands, and preferred to have guys as her friends. She got pregnant when she was still in high school. She ended up marrying the guy and had my niece by the time she was eighteen.

He husband was abusive. I would get calls in the middle of the night to come and get her. Once I walked in their house and she was cowering with her daughter in her arms, her husband angrily threatening to hit her. Each time, I'd take her to my house and a couple of days later I'd get a call at work: "We got back together." It made me so angry. They did drugs and drank together. Then she'd stop and try to get him to stop, too. That's when he would start beating her.

She finally got out of that marriage and then got right into another one. My mom and dad helped them buy a house. It couldn't have been but three or four months after they moved in that I got a call. He was threatening to hit her, she said. He was pulling things off the wall and breaking them. When I went there, it was just a mess. He had totaled the house. Some friends helped me kick him out.

My parents asked me to move in with Barb to help with the house payments. I had to give notice on my house – I had the cutest little beach cottage – so it was four weeks before I could move in. The morning that I came into the house with my boxes, I opened the door and there was a mattress on the living room floor with a strange guy sleeping on it. Excuse me? Here we go again, I thought.

This new guy was highly educated, a Harvard graduate. They'd met through the company they both worked for. She was doing some computer work for the corporation. He was in the management hierarchy.

He was controlling. I saw it while living in the house with them. Before too long, I started staying with friends. I would still stay with my sister and her boyfriend a couple of nights a week to keep an eye on my niece who was five years old by then. I loved her dearly and tried to give her some normalcy. My sister was doing a lot of drinking. I didn't know it at the time, but she was also doing Quaaludes and cocaine.

One morning, I was walking down the hallway and the bathroom door opened. My niece came out wrapped in a towel and my sister's boyfriend was behind her, also wrapped in a towel. He had given my niece a shower. I came unglued. I lost it. They threw me out of the house. It wasn't pretty. I called my other sisters because I felt that they needed to know what was going on. I told them Barb was drinking and possibly using drugs. I told them I didn't trust her boyfriend. About a week later we had a meeting and decided that we were all going to come to the house together to do an intervention.

Her boyfriend accused me of making everything up. But my sister started crying and admitted that she had a problem. She didn't want to go to rehab at first, but we insisted and she finally agreed to go to an in-patient program that we had pre-arranged. We couldn't see her for the first 10 days. Then we went with her to counseling. A lot of things came out in counseling about her anger towards us, about her feeling abandoned as a child. Her anger was directed at us, not at our parents, but at the siblings.

We told her boyfriend to stay away, but he came to all of the counseling sessions. He listened and came around to admitting that she did have a drinking problem. We vented some of our own anger towards him during the sessions, too, for having denied the problem before, for having lied to us.

When Barb got out of rehab, she went back to living with her boyfriend and he became husband number three. He had a successful career and they moved from the little three-bedroom bungalow in West LA to a beautiful, stately, brand-new home in the Anaheim Hills. Now isolated from her family, my sister started drinking again. No one knew it was happening. She didn't have any friends. Her husband didn't want her to work and became more and more controlling. He told her what to wear. He bought all of her clothes.

She didn't tell us what was happening at the time, but the relationship deteriorated and she eventually left him. Packed up her daughter who was now eight and moved to Alaska. She'd gotten a job up there through someone she knew. We don't know the entire story of what happened up there, but we know that she continued on a downward spiral.

As time went on, Barb would come down and visit our parents and they would go up to see her. She was struggling financially. You could tell that things just weren't right with her. She would send out these crazy broadcast emails late at night. You could tell she was drunk. That went on for a couple of years. When she'd come to town, she'd act like everything was fine, but we kind of knew what was going on. Her daughter would visit in the summer, but never shared any details about what her home life was like.

In 2004, our dad's health took a bad turn. He had congestive heart failure and there were no more medical treatments left. We moved a hospital bed into the den, right where his chair had been for 55 years, and brought him home so he could be with family where he wanted to be. Barb came down from Alaska. The first couple of days we were all busy because there was so much to take care of, but soon we started to notice her odd behavior. She would talk very loudly and in a high-pitched voice. One night she told us, "I'm making dinner. Dinner will be on the table," but at 4 o'clock, she was nowhere to be found. We found a box of wine, almost empty. We figured out that she had been pouring it into a Pepsi can to hide her drinking.

Her behavior became more and more obnoxious and erratic. Our dad had lost consciousness at this point and after several of us discussed it, one of my older sisters told her, "Look, we're putting you on a plane." We called her husband — her fourth husband, a good guy, but someone we didn't really know — and told him that we were sending her home, that she was out-of-control, that she was drinking.

When she got home, she sent out a broadcast email to everybody in our family saying that we were keeping her away from her parents. She claimed that Dad had told her we had ripped off money from him.

Our dad passed a few days later and Barb came back to California for the funeral. She stood back, didn't say much, and didn't stay long. To us, she seemed more angry than embarrassed.

As it turns out, after all of this, her husband did get her some help that included counseling through their church and AA meetings, which he attended with her. Barb came down to see all of us again and to repair some of the damage that she had done. She confessed all of the things that she had done, like sleeping with one of my boyfriends. It was a lot of things like that.

She also told us about having been date-raped in high school. We didn't understand why she hadn't come to us when it happened. We were like Mama Bears, her big sisters. We would have gone crazy on this guy. She said that she hadn't because she didn't think we would have believed her, that we would have thought she was just trying to get attention. How could she think that? How many times had I come to her house when she called me to come get her after she was beat-up?

All of us were just so taken aback by that. We were so out of touch with what she had been going through.

By the time my mom passed in 2008, our sister had been sober for four years. She came down again and really helped us out this time, sorting through family photos and separating them so that everyone got their own set.

Through counseling, family support, and hard work, she has gotten her life back on track. In the years between our dad and mom passing, she came down periodically for two weeks at a time to do stuff around their house for Mom and visit with us sisters. Sometimes her husband would come with her. He did a lot of repairs and such at my mom's house. We got to know him better, too.

None of us had ever gone to Alaska, so after our mom died, one of my sisters and I went up there. We had so much fun. Her house felt like a home. We told funny old stories that showed the positive side of our life growing up. We shared little tidbits about what it had been like when our parents had visited each of our homes. We cooked together, experimenting with new recipes. We met her friends from church and spent time with her husband, who clearly adores her. Our sister acted as tour guide; we did a tour of the fjords where we saw bears and went salmon fishing. She was so happy to share her life and community with us.

There were family members - especially the brothers - who took a long time to believe that she could really be fine now because of all of the stuff that she did. Slowly but surely she's rebuilt a relationship with everybody, though. She keeps in contact with the extended family, inquiring about them, keeping up on family milestones. My siblings and I now have a standing Friday afternoon group phone call. Any of the 10 of us that are available joins in on the call, and Barb is often part of them. Now it's a real relationship.

She looks fantastic these days and is in better shape than all of us. She loves being out on the water and the solace she finds there, with the deep blue glacial water and the eagles flying over. She's involved in a whole lot of groups now, is involved with her church, and goes to the gym. She's found things that she takes pleasure in doing.

A couple of years ago Barb had to have major hip surgery. She was concerned about taking the prescribed pain medication and only took it for the first three days after the surgery, when the pain was at its worst. She's so much better now, but for a while after the surgery when we would call and ask how she was, she'd tell us that she'd had a bad night. That it hurt a lot. But she stayed away from the pain pills.

Barb doesn't go to AA anymore, but we don't talk about that. She says that she drank to mask her feelings, but once she was able to confront them and deal with her past, she no longer felt the urge to drink like she had before. It doesn't rule her life now.

Our Thoughts

Today, the signs of trauma and abuse are more widely known, but back when Barb was raped, her entire family missed the evidence. With no one close to confide in, Barb kept it to herself, compounding the trauma with a profound sense of isolation. She had been popular in school, but after the rape, dropped her female friendships and became flirty and promiscuous. Instead of exploring the underlying cause of this abrupt personality shift, the siblings looked only at the behavior. With a brood of 10 children, her parents may well have been suffering a degree of parental fatigue or assumed that the older siblings were keeping an eye on Barb, their youngest, as parental surrogates.

As her personal problems became more apparent, her family became hyper-involved in Barb's personal business. The approach they used was to bail her out of bad relationships rather than draw her out and help her understand and deal with the reasons behind her bad choices.

There are many factors that contributed to Barb's ultimate sobriety, primarily her own resolve and Barb's fourth (and current) husband. Theresa did not share, and may not know, if he precipitated Barb's sobriety through ultimatums or showered her with unconditional love and support, but he clearly played a big part in helping her find her footing and turn her life around. Also, the AA meetings, connecting with her community, and being able to finally trust her siblings enough to share her dark secrets made it possible to develop the closeness with her family she had longed for all of her life.

Theresa had to work through some guilt issues of her own. She wishes that Barb had felt safe enough to tell her about the rape when it happened and feels intense guilt knowing that Barb was afraid that she wouldn't have believed her. She's had to take a hard look at herself from her sister's perspective and see that, for all of her rescuing and intervening, she also undermined Barb's self-confidence and self-worth by treating her as the little sister who needed to be looked after.

Barb's alcoholism has taken a toll on all family members. It took two of the brothers a long time to get over their anger toward Barb for all that the family went through because of her drinking and the spillover of her personal drama into their lives.

Shame, embarrassment, and guilt are all powerful triggers for alcoholics. It takes a lot of fortitude and resolve to stay sober in the long climb back to respectability. Barb is lucky to also have her extended family. Where once the long reach of family was something that held her down, it is now part of what lifts her up.

MISPLAYING A BAD HAND
Judy's Story

Obstinate denial is one brother's chosen defense for a trifecta of strikes against him: early trauma, strong cultural influences and heredity.

The only person who doesn't know my brother is an alcoholic is my brother. Ben is clueless. His alcohol is the primary relationship in his life. That mistress, alcohol, destroyed two marriages to two lovely women, both of whom were absolutely wild about him, and both of whom finally left full of bitterness.

I'm the oldest of the siblings; Ben is two years younger. We grew up during the 40's and 50's in Bakersfield, California; a time when professional men like my father were still doing three-martini lunches, and when socializing was at home, small dinner parties and such, where the husbands drank liberally (the wives less so). There was never any sense that there was something wrong with that. It was a different culture at that time. That was the model my brother had.

When my brother was 14, we suffered a family tragedy. The family, minus my dad who was on a hunting trip, was on a church-organized outing in the country. My sisters, ages five and seven, became bored and went back to the car. Mom went wandering in one direction. I was chatting with friends. Ben had crossed the main road and was waiting with a small group for others to join them when my five-year-old sister came running out into the road. She was struck by a passing vehicle and dragged. She died at the scene.

Each of us felt responsible for not having kept her safe that day and carried the weight of our guilt heavily. My mother, unable to handle her grief, turned on my brother, blaming him for not watching out for his sister. Her own health and life collapsed at that point. She had always been fragile. She ended up with a decade-long drug problem and was in and out of mental hospitals until she finally committed suicide with drugs. Ben managed to make his way through college, and then joined the military. He ended up running the officer's club on the base. He was in his thirties by that time and drinking heavily. There was a lot of drinking on the base. Ben and his wife were barely speaking, in large part because of the way he treated her when he had been drinking. When he didn't have alcohol in his system he was as sweet as he could be, but after a few beers, he became belligerent and incredibly aggressive toward women.

He had a succession of jobs after leaving the military. He got a sales job and conducted his business at the bars. Always drinking. He was fired from that job. Then he lost a wholesale/retail fish business that he financed by borrowing tons of money from Dad. It was a business he should and could have made a great success because he was himself a fisherman. He'd been in the area a long time. He had the connections. But he left his employees to run the store while he drank at the bars, "making sales." He drank up the profits, and the business suffered from his neglect.

He is retired now and a barely-functioning alcoholic. He gets up at five in the morning, runs his dog behind his pickup, and by nine o'clock he's in the bar and drinking one pitcher of beer after the other. By about five o'clock he comes home. He eats and he says he goes to bed early. But I know he passes out.

Our sister and I have learned that if we're going to have any conversation with him, it has to be before ten in the morning, before he's gotten started on his beer. And if he calls us later in the day, unless we want it to turn into a raging, angry diatribe, we don't challenge or contradict or try to direct the conversation in any way. We stay as neutral as possible.

He has no friends. He had his favorite bars when he first moved to Washington after he retired. Then he had a couple of different favorites. By the time my sister and I went up for a visit, after he'd been there for four or five years, he was doing most of his drinking in the next town over. He has been 86'd from a lot of bars because, when he's drunk, he gets aggressive and mean towards his waitresses. It's not that he's sexually aggressive, he's just mean. If she doesn't do something his way, he shouts, he yells, might throw beer on her. And I know of at least two cases where he got in fights with men in bars.

My brother has four children; they have all disowned him. He tells this pathetic story about how badly his oldest daughter and her husband treated him when he went back east to see his grandchildren. He says that his daughter was terrible to him and that her husband physically threw him of the house. He has done his best to demonize her to the rest of family.

Ben's son Kyle, who is also an alcoholic, moved to Washington to spend some time with his father, to reconnect and sort out his own life. He was going to AA meetings and trying to stay sober. His sponsor told him he should not live with his dad because, of course, his dad was still drinking. Kyle has stayed in the area, but has his own place now.

Ben has another daughter, the youngest child, who is addicted to drugs. Ben was her hero and she's repeating many of his dysfunctional patterns. And there's one other daughter who's got it together. She and her husband have a strong religious base and a bunch of kids. Ben was thrilled when she and her family also moved nearby and visited them often at first. But then, drunk, he went outside in front of her house and peed against a tree. She doesn't want her children exposed to that behavior. Like my sister and me, his daughter now tells him, "If you want to visit, you need to visit us before nine a.m." Before his daily drinking begins.

My husband used to go fishing with Ben. On their last trip they weren't able to go out because the weather was bad. My brother managed to go the first few days without drinking. He could do that. By the fourth day he said, "Let me show you where I hang out. Let me show you what my day is like." My husband said that the pub they went to was a really down-heeled place. My brother had three pitchers of beer by noon.

The next time my husband and I were up there, the family all went out for breakfast. My brother said to us, "Everybody thinks I drink, but this is what I do in the morning. I don't drink." He said to my husband, "Remember that time you came up to go fishing and we couldn't go out because of the bad weather and we just hung out?"

Maybe my brother doesn't remember, which is certainly possible, or maybe he just rewrites life. Like his reality and everyone else's reality are on different channels.

Frankly, I'm surprised my brother reached 65. He smokes non-stop. He has heart trouble. He's obese. He has gout. And he drinks himself to bed every night. He's been at this for so long, I don't see how he can change. If I could have a really open and candid conversation with my brother today, I would tell him that I love him. I would talk to him about that traumatic day when our younger sister was killed. I would tell him that the person I keep in my heart and my mind is the little boy he once was. I would tell him, "When you are sober, you are that person again. You are sweet and kind and loving, but after the first pitcher of beer, you become someone completely different. And it's someone I don't want to be around. Someone I'm afraid of. And I deeply grieve the loss of the person I loved."

I would say, "You are the only person in this family that does not know that alcohol controls your life, and it prevents you from having close relationships with family and others. I would help you if I could but only you can deal with this and it has to be something you want to do." I have tried to have this conversation with him, but the minute I say, "alcohol" he snaps back, "I don't drink that much."

I've done genome work for other health issues that shows that, from both my parents, I have a marker that predisposes me toward depression, alcoholism, and drug abuse. It's a bio-chemical imbalance. There is alcoholism on my father's side of the family. My great grandfather died of binge drinking. All four male cousins have battled with alcoholism. My brother sees none of that as relevant to him. When I tried to share with him what I have learned about genomes, his response was, "That's great Sis, that you learned that about you, but it has nothing to do with me."

I think the reason that I escaped the family pattern of alcohol abuse is because of several vivid Technicolor memories of my mother heavily on drugs, which were so horrifying to me that I vowed not to look like that. I was not going to let that be me.

It took a lot to come to terms with the notion that I cannot fix this person. All I can do is love him and pray for him. And hope that whatever spirits are in the world will keep him safe and that he won't hurt himself or someone else.

Our Thoughts

While sharing her story, Judy mentioned numerous times that she had accepted the fact that she couldn't help her brother — that he didn't want to change, or even acknowledge that he needed to change – and she had come to terms with that reality. As we talked, though, I could hear the strain of suppressed emotion in her voice. She admitted that she wasn't quite as OK with things as she had believed.

Judy has given a great deal of thought to the factors that contributed to Ben's drinking: the shared family trauma, the culture in which he was raised and the inherited genome markers. She speculates that his anger at his mother in blaming him for his sister's death is behind his ill treatment of women. His drunkenness either depresses his normal filters of civility, allowing him to lash out at waitresses and wives, or he simply uses his drunkenness as an excuse to behave so badly.

Birth order probably plays into the dynamics of this relationship. Being the oldest of the siblings with a mother who was, at best, unavailable to her children, Judy no doubt felt a sense of responsibility to her younger brother and sister. In addition to her comprehensive understanding of the reasons that led to Ben's drinking, she also has a great deal of sisterly compassion for him.

Judy has spent over 35 years practicing tough love, setting boundaries and showing compassion. She works on letting go, but hope is a hard thing to surrender.

WAITING FOR THE INEVITABLE
Trisha's Story

Trisha has tried to help her sister get sober for three decades. She has read volumes of self-help books and attended Al-Anon. Cutting ties with her sister has been painful and second-guessing herself a battle.

※

My dad died at 59, the same age my younger sister Jo is right now. For the life of me, I don't know why she's still alive.

With my dad, I held on to the hope that some day he would stop drinking. And then he died and I realized that it was never going to be different. And it might very well be that way with my sister. It's one of those things that you have to come to terms with, but I don't think that I'm prepared for the day she goes.

My dad was an alcoholic my whole life. He said he started drinking at age 13. He and my mom got married when she was 15 and he was 17. They stayed married until he passed away, but it was an unhappy marriage, a dysfunctional marriage. My dad never finished eighth grade. He worked a little, but mom was the breadwinner.

Back in those days, my mother did everything that the perfect wife was supposed to do. Honor and love your husband. She felt that was the life she was dealt.

My dad also mentally abused my mom, undermined her self-confidence. She believed she couldn't make a life on her own.

He was verbally abusive to me, physically abusive to my brother, and mentally abusive to my mother. Jo says he was sexually abusive to her, but her stories have been getting more convoluted as time goes by. I don't know if he would have done anything like that, but there was a lot of abuse. When we would get spanked, it would be with the buckle end of the belt.

I had a friend whose father was a banker. I remember seeing the mom reach up and give the dad a kiss. Everything at their home was just love and joy and happiness and talking and laughter. Ours was a home full of silence. We watched TV. There were never any conversations. I knew that there was something better than this, that even though my life was such hell God was showing me what the other side looked like – that my life could be better and different. That was something that I always hung on to.

I can only remember one noteworthy conversation with my dad. One. I was 38 at the time and I was taking care of him while my mom went to Texas to visit her sister. I said, "Dad, if you had to do it all over again, would you change anything?" And he goes, "Nope."

Mind you, he was missing a leg and missing a foot. They'd amputated because of Vasculitus Articulitus, all due to drinking and smoking. He had never tried to walk after that. He couldn't take care of himself and seemed like he'd just given up. Just ready to die. This was two or three years before he passed away.

I asked him, "You would still drink at 13? You would still smoke at 13? You wouldn't change any of that?"

"Nope. I could have stopped if I wanted to. I didn't want to."

When he died the minister asked us if there was anything we wanted to say about him at the funeral, anything we wanted to share and we said no.

After dad passed, Mom went to bereavement counseling, and she came back and she said, "Honey, I learned something new today. Did you know that we were a dysfunctional family?" This was something we never talked about before. She had never talked to her friends about her relationship with Dad or what was happening. It wasn't that she was holding a secret; she didn't realize that this wasn't how other people lived.

I did a lot of self-help stuff in my 30's. I read *Co-dependency No More* and *Healing the Child Within*, and started going to group counseling for adult children of alcoholics. I was trying to understand about alcoholism in the family and the damage it causes, and get some support.

My sister never did any of that. She goes to AA, even now, but I don't believe she ever made it to step four (making a searching and fearless moral inventory of ourselves). I think she goes because she doesn't want people to think she drinks.

In some ways, Jo and I were close when we were growing up. We shared a room until she got married. I think we knew each other as best as people can know another, good and bad, but it was never with deep caring that I see other sisters have.

Jo acted manipulative and vindictive toward me. She took three of my boyfriends in high school. Because she was beautiful she seemed to think she could get anything she wanted.

In her early adult years, she did really, really, well financially. She flaunted all her fine jewelry, bragging about how much this cost and how much that cost.

She had a terrible first marriage. Her husband introduced her to diet pills and other prescription drugs, and beat her. She had two miscarriages.

I first recognized that she had a drinking problem after she married her second husband. She would tell me she was going in late to work because she worked so late the night before but then I'd find out she stayed up all night drinking. On Saturday mornings she would clean the house with a tumbler of wine.

Over the next few years, she got divorced, married again, and then left that husband for her boss. They moved across the country together, but it wasn't long before she came back to California.

That's when it started to get bad. Really bad.

She would call and talk incessantly for hours. She seemed really paranoid and appeared to be hallucinating. She would tell the same story over and over again. My mom and I would try to help her solve her problems and then find out she didn't even remember the conversations where we'd discussed them. It got to where we thought we were the crazy ones.

She went through many rehabilitation programs, primarily alcohol recovery, but there was always a mental health component, too. She would do fine in a facility without drinking for a short period of time, but six months was probably the longest period without a drink.

Jo lived on the streets. She lived with friends. She was in a halfway house. At one point we were out of her life for maybe two years.

When she re-appeared, we learned she had been diagnosed with bipolar disorder. We set her up in a motel, and then helped get her into a one-year rehab program. After less than six months, she just walked out and got on a bus. We didn't know where she was for three days or so.

One night, she was left alone at our home for a little bit and got into our liquor cabinet. She had a mini-stroke, and had to go to the hospital not even being able to swallow. After that, she had to be in a wheelchair for a while.

Jo now lives on her own. She doesn't work, and lives in public housing. The police have been called three times to her place. When my sister drinks, she gets mean and belligerent, to us and to her neighbors.

She's angry with us because we won't take care of her in the way she wants to be taken care of. She wants us to do everything for her and if we won't she'll start harassing us. I used to get phone calls, 20 calls a night, where she'd be talking angrily to my voice mail.

My mom and I have told Jo we will help her any way we can, but if she chooses to drink, we can't have anything to do with her. There has to be a cutoff. We can't live the craziness. If we let her come to all the holidays so she'll be happy, everyone around her will be miserable. As Christians we are supposed to be there and lift everyone up, but I struggle with it.

I tried many times to have a real conversation with my sister to express my love, my compassion, my heartache of seeing her suffer like she does. And to let her know that I'd like to have a relationship with her. I'm always praying for her and her wellbeing. It is her choice to stay away.

I have had no contact with my sister for over a year now. I feel guilty. I do pay for her phone service though, so at least I know she has some source of help by having the phone.

By not having a relationship with her, is it not having a relationship with alcohol or not having a relationship with the sister? I don't know the difference. I struggle with how much how much this is a disease of the mind, a mental problem. Do you get angry with someone who is sick? No. But do you allow that sick person to make you sick? I've done that for so many years.

My regret is that my family — my kids, my husband — had to witness the turmoil. I was so in the middle of it I couldn't understand the pain that it put them through. If I could do anything over again, I would have been more ballsy. I would have said, "Enough" sooner and left. But I stuck it out, hoping – that insanity part of doing the same thing over and over again and expecting a different result – things would change.

I keep saying that she's like a cat with nine lives and she's seen ten. I believe God has kept her alive for a reason, for something. Is it about her getting it right before she dies? Is it a lesson for someone else? I don't know.

Our Thoughts

Talk about being caught in the middle. Trisha wants to protect her mother, her family and herself from the fallout of her sister's alcoholism and mental health issues, but, at the same time, wants to uphold what she believes to be her Christian moral responsibilities.

Pushing back on the unhappiness of growing up in a dysfunctional household, both Trisha and Jo actively sought out a different life for themselves as adults. Trisha craved normalcy, loving relationships, and assurance of a higher purpose in this life. Jo was drawn toward material trappings and constantly sought reassurance of her desirability.

Trisha read self-help books, went to church, and attended Al-anon meetings; Jo drank and showed little regard for the impact her behavior had on others.

It took many years for Trisha to accept that she could not save Jo and only when she began fearing for her mother's safety was she able to shift her priorities to self-preservation instead of futilely trying to change Jo's behavior. She continues to pray for her sister's wellbeing and struggles with her resolve to stay away, but understands both intellectually and in her heart that she has made to right decision. Sometimes we don't get a happy ending. We do all that we can do and then try our best to let go.

Spouses
married to an alcoholic

In a marriage with an alcoholic, the balance of power typically tilts to the drinker while the bulk of responsibility shifts heavily to the sober partner. Instead of a healthy, equal relationship, one spouse can be forced into the role of caregiver, burdened with cleaning up the other's messes both literally and figuratively.

The alcoholic's frequent inability (or refusal) to share in family obligations and their unreliable and erratic behavior can cause debilitating anxiety for their spouse. Faced with a loss of control in their marriage and in their home, the spouse is constantly forced into a position of reacting to the chaos that the drinking partner causes. Even in relatively good times, the non-alcoholic spouse can be highly stressed, waiting for the other shoe to drop.

If this describes your situation, it may not be possible to discuss your concern about the drinking without triggering a negative response. But this is something you must do in order to take back control of your life. Be supportive of the drinker's efforts to get sober, and firm with your resolve not to enable. Set boundaries. The more self-confident you feel, the less power your partner holds over you. Take back your life.

DRINKING BUDDIES
Val's Story

It's hard for Terry to be a responsible family man when he can't seem to resist keeping up with the guys when the drinks start flowing. For this husband, finding a way to hold on to those friendships and maintain sobriety hasn't been easy.

※

Terry had a few neighbor buddies, Dean in particular, whose houses he would go to every Monday night, like clockwork, to watch football. He would come home stumbling drunk. Then he started going over for Sunday football, also. It was close enough for him to walk, so I didn't have to worry about him driving drunk, but a couple of times he was so blitzed that Dean and his wife had to drive him home. He was too drunk to walk. He would get his act together for work, though, and wouldn't drink much during the week. This was the pattern for a few years.

Little by little, Terry's drinking became a daily ritual. His heaviest drinking years began in earnest when our son, Sean, was in fifth grade and daughter, Heather, was in fourth grade and continued for about five challenging years.

One time, when Heather was eleven and Sean was twelve, the kids were flying home after a summer visit to their cousin's farm. Terry drove down to LAX to pick them up. He met them on time at the gate, got them on the parking lot shuttle, but then couldn't find the car. Sean called me, really upset, from the airport parking lot. He said, "Mom. I think Dad is drunk. He can't find the car. He can't remember where he parked it."

That was a hard moment for me. I was in Santa Barbara, at least two hours away. I knew the kids were scared. I told Sean, "After you find the car, don't let Dad drive for at least an hour. You have to keep the keys from him. Tell him to take a nap in the car. Promise me that you'll do that." I talked to Terry, too. I told him to sleep it off. They made it home safely later that evening. I laid down a dictum that he was no longer allowed to drive with the kids in the car.

I took the kids to a few meetings of Teen Al-Anon to help them deal with their father's alcoholism. Adults are normally excluded from the meetings so that the teens will feel freer to share openly, but Sean and Heather were the youngest kids in the room and I insisted on staying. We had talked between us about their dad's drinking and I felt that they would be OK talking in front of me. Heather had already told me about how she could tell that he had been drinking when he came to her volleyball games because he acted goofy. It really embarrassed her. I think both kids benefited by going to Al-Anon. They heard other teens tell their stories. During the meetings, others would talk about how their own dad or mom had come home sloppy drunk and I would see how Sean and Heather would nod their heads.

Terry and I had heart-to-heart discussions about whether we should stay together. Neither of us are confrontational people by nature. We managed to keep the dialog civil, but for all the conversations — me laying out my fears about him getting into an accident some day, how his drinking embarrassed the children and how much we all worried about him — not much changed.

I took the children to a session with a family counselor. I felt that they needed a place where they could talk to somebody who could provide better answers than I was able to. It was a big mistake all around. Heather wouldn't talk. Sean told the therapist that his father was always drinking. The day after the session, the counselor called me and demanded that we come back for another appointment and that Terry had to come, also, or he would report our family to protective services and they would take the kids from us. We came and Terry said all the right things; he acknowledged that he had a drinking problem and agreed to check himself into Serenity House, a local rehab facility. The threat of losing our children was averted. We did not have any further dealings with that counselor, though. There was no trust between him and us.

Serenity House offered a couple of short-term options. Terry stayed just a few nights and then attended a handful of AA meetings afterwards. Less than a month later, he got picked up for drunk driving. He was not sentenced to jail time, but the experience of being arrested and the several hours he spent in jail while being processed was a humiliating experience for him. He quit drinking cold turkey and really got his life back under control.

Terry stayed sober for four or five years, and then one weekend his old drinking buddy, Dean, was back in town for a visit, and he couldn't resist the temptation to drink. Terry got so drunk that another friend, Bob, had to bring him home. I refused to let him in. I told him to go back to Bob's and sleep it off. I don't think he drank again for quite a long time, four years at least, after that.

And then, a little over a year ago, John, one of Terry's best friends, was diagnosed with cancer which required aggressive treatment of chemo and radiation. Dean, who was also a tight friend of John's, came back down. All of the families were going to have a big dinner together. Terry went earlier than I and was already completely inebriated by the time I arrived. It amazed me that Terry's friends didn't think it was a big deal. They all knew that Terry was an alcoholic. Terry tried to excuse himself, saying that it was because of John's cancer; they just wanted to have a party before he started treatment. I told him, "Fine. That's your decision, but you aren't coming home."

Later on we had a conversation about the kind of example he was for Sean who had developed his own drinking problems. I said, "Sean is working on being sober and then he sees you drunk and trying to justify it because your friend is ill."

Three months ago, I suspected that he'd been drinking again. We had friends from out-of-town staying with us and I knew that they were drinking. I didn't actually see Terry drinking with them, but he has his 'tells.' When he's been drinking, he'll chew a mouthful of gum, not just a piece or two. He won't kiss me right on the lips. He'll act goofy. He stands differently, like he's on shipboard and trying to maintain his balance.

I found a bottle of vodka in his golf bag. Then sure enough, I found more bottles in a black bag tucked up under the seat in his car along with two cups. I could smell the alcohol in the cups.

I had to decide what I was going to do. I took a walk with a good friend who knew my history. Terry can articulate his positions very well to justify what he does, or doesn't, do. I went through the arguments with my friend, like the fact that I sometimes drink wine. The difference is that I don't hide it and I don't drink and drive.

The next morning, I lined the vodka bottles up on the table by his side of the bed and then left for work. That night, confronted with the evidence of his drinking, Terry tried to put me on the defensive by showing outrage that I went through his car. I wasn't going to let him put this on me. It wasn't about me. I told him, "That's beside the point. It looks like you are drinking and driving – again. And putting everything at risk – again."

"I don't have the answers, but you need to figure it out. Go to an AA meeting or somewhere else to get help. There are plenty of other resources available. It's on you to do whatever it takes to stay sober. I don't know what the trigger was that caused you to go off the wagon, but Terry, clearly, when you hide booze in your car, you know what you are doing isn't right."

So, that's where we've left it for now. I really don't know if he'll turn it around again or not. It's still an ongoing process for me. I take things as they come and try to figure it out as I go.

Our Thoughts

Val had to weigh complicated, opposing factors in deciding whether to stay with Terry. Most seriously, there were the drinking and driving incidents that put himself and innocent people, particularly their children, in harm's way. Val also had to weigh the value of the generally positive and loving bond between the children and Terry against the role model he had become with his drunkenness as the children were entering the impressionable teen years.

Val says she did not leave Terry because she believed that he had the capacity to control his drinking. She still loved him and knew that he loved his family. She did not want to give up on a person she loved. At the same time, she and the kids attended Al-Anon meetings and took other measures in preparation for leaving Terry if he continued to drink.

The kids are now young adults. Val and Terry are still together. Terry is sober most of the time, although Val knows of a few lapses and suspects that there are other drinking escapades outside of her knowledge. She calls him out when she sees evidence of drinking and is clear on her intention to leave if he reverts back to his former drinking behavior.

Val's life is a constant sea of conflicting emotions: hope, distrust, love and resolve. Terry will never fully regain Val's trust until he completely gives up alcohol. Until or unless that day comes, we agree that Val should keep an exit strategy in mind.

A SELFISH MAN
Diana's Story

Diagnosis and treatment of mental illness was even more challenging 40 years ago than it is today. When the husband in this story was finally diagnosed with manic depression, the treatment was large doses of lithium and no counseling or other support for him or his family. Self medicating with alcohol further complicated this couple's relationship.

When I met my husband Jake, who was five years older than I, he was a married man. He was an impulsive man and I was head over heels in love. He got a rushed annulment and we were married very soon after that. I had just turned nineteen.

Jake spent those first years of our marriage going to college and working. We had our first child ten months after our wedding and then two more babies, one after another. We lived in student housing not far from my parents in San Diego. My mother helped a lot so I could go to college myself. I went to classes as often as I could and worked as a waitress off and on.

I was pretty feisty. My family was very political and I was taken on marches starting when I was four years old. That was my initial attraction to my husband. We met working on the Henry Wallace campaign for president and later became very involved in the civil rights movement and anti-war movement. Two of the biggest issues of the day for us were the Rosenbergs, who were accused of spying for the Soviet Union, and Emmett Till, the African-American teenager who was lynched for allegedly flirting with a white woman. We were involved in lots of other campaigns, too, around a lot of issues. I took my own kids on marches when they were very young.

That was during the McCarthy anti-communist period. My husband was subpoenaed because he had been in the Communist Party – and actually kicked out of the Communist Party. He was too far to the left, even for them.

We moved to L.A. after the FBI investigation. Jake was able to keep his job with the railroad. He had already graduated from college but he was more interested in being involved in political things than going out and finding a job in his field – he majored in industrial arts, astronomy and sociology. Three majors. He was very, very smart. He never did pursue a career that utilized his degrees or his potential. He was a nonconformist who couldn't follow other people's rules. He had to work on his own.

Early in our relationship some of our mutual political friends told me that they were concerned with what they called my husband's erratic behavior, but we were young and in love and passionate about so many issues. I was not worried about his idiosyncrasies. Alcohol was never an issue during that time. Sometimes my father would barbeque and he and Jake would have a beer together, but that was about it. I never saw any indication that alcohol was going to be a problem.

By the time the children were getting older and starting school, we needed a bigger house. Friends of ours had moved to a small city just east of LA and told us there was a house for rent around the corner from them — a big house, three bedrooms, that was right across the street from a school. So we followed them out there.

I went to work at a nursery school. Jake worked the night shift at the railroad and worked days house painting as a journeyman painter. Non-union. He had been in the Painters Union when I met him, but was kicked out of the union because of his political activities. It was hard without the G.I. bill anymore. Even though Jake had always worked, the G.I. bill had kind of supported us. Housing had been very inexpensive with the G.I. allowance. Now our expenses were getting greater. We stopped going to political meetings or out to dinner.

I found out that Jake had affairs and I was dumb and naïve enough to blame myself. I was too busy with the children; too busy working, I told myself. So I excused his behavior. Jake became domineering and controlling. He started bringing home a six-pack of beer every night. In the time between one job and the next, he needed to have a couple of beers to relax, he said. And then, when he came home from the second job, he would drink some more.

That's when I became concerned. He only drank beer, but he needed huge quantities to get the effect he wanted. When I brought it up with him, he pooh-poohed me and got defensive. He just needed to relax. Wasn't he working hard enough? It's not like he was going out to bars.

One day Jake was mowing the lawn and caught his foot under the blades. He had to go to the hospital, and they gave him a tetanus shot and a cortisone shot. That's when he had his first breakdown. Mental breakdown. He began to hallucinate during that stay at the hospital. I don't know if he had been having hallucinations before that time, but it was the first time I knew about it. I was so frightened. I knew he was going to be discharged from the hospital and I didn't know what was going to happen. The doctors were treating his delusions as a temporary reaction to the trauma and medications. I had a very dear friend who was a psychiatric social worker and she told me about a psychiatric hospital in L.A. We were able to persuade Jake to sign himself into that hospital. He was there for about six weeks.

Jake liked the feeling he experienced when he was hallucinating. He had a sense of power. He built up fantasies. When he came down from it he was really depressed. He was diagnosed with manic depression, which is now called bipolar disorder. It was what his dad had, although I did not know it at the time.

There was so little knowledge about bipolar disorder back then and not a lot of support from the hospital for the patient or their families. Jake hated his medications and hated the side effects. Drinking was his choice of medicine. It made him feel better. At that time, they used heavy medications – haloperidol.

My parents sensed what was going on. I tried not to involve them. I didn't want them to know. Jake seemed to be keeping his condition under control for the most part and I wanted to be able to be independent.

In 1959, when I was 29 years old, we saw an ad for a school for sale in the newspaper. The landlady was willing to lease the building to us. It was a situation where we could actually move into one building and run the school out of the other building. My mother and dad, my mother particularly, came through with enough money for the initial cost – $3,000 – so we went into business and my husband made it a beautiful facility. He was very handy. He could fix anything.

The school began to thrive but Jake's drinking didn't slow down. He lost his job with the railroad because he decided on our 14th wedding anniversary he wanted the night off and told them he wasn't coming in. He had a friend who was able to get him another job driving a truck, and we struggled along. Meanwhile, he had another major affair, which was devastating for me. I felt that he was my fourth child sometimes. He behaved like a child, self-centered and was careless about how what he did or said impacted anyone else.

The kids were growing up and becoming more and more aware of their fathers drinking. He now also went out to bars to play pool and we never knew when he was going to come home. I got used to it. He became overweight, developed a beer belly and began to care less and less about his appearance. Jake had been a very handsome young man but he no longer was as attractive. The affairs ended once he began to drink heavily.

At home he was moody and erratic I never knew whom I was going to wake up to in the morning. Every day could be different. He had been an involved father, but now he worked nights and was not around to spend evenings with the kids.

The drinking was a secret. I wanted to appear as normal as possible. The staff at the school kind of knew what was going on and were extremely supportive of me. They felt that he was abusive. There was abuse, but it was more emotional abuse. He berated me for the way I was running the school. I was too easy. I wasn't demanding payment from parents. I wasn't tough enough on the teachers. I spoiled them. That kind of thing. But I kept plodding along.

I always felt that my husband was not a bad person. He was a sick person. He had a strong work ethic and he gave that work ethic to our children. He involved the boys in maintenance work at the school on Saturdays. It was tough on them but he taught them a lot, also.

My parents, no matter what, were always there for us. They smothered him with love and acceptance. I tried not to tell them. I lived in L.A. They lived in San Diego. I tried not to involve them in what I was going through. I really kept it a big secret as long as I could. It was a secret from our friends. It had to be kept a secret in those days, particularly owning a preschool and having the responsibility of all those children. Keeping everybody safe. Nobody could know. As far as they were concerned, I was always fine. Only, sometimes my staff knew. And as I say, they were especially supportive. Some of them stayed with me twenty years. We ran a good school.

I worried about my husband. I always felt responsible for him, for his safety. He took lithium for a long time. He saw a psychiatrist for the medications, but he never went for counseling. They would just give blood tests to make sure the lithium levels were balanced. Eventually he lost his trucking job, but he was old enough to retire by then.

Eventually, we reached a point, after the kids had gone, when we just didn't see a lot of each other. We worked out a schedule where we didn't have a lot of contact. He was gone nights, I was gone days. We no longer had a real marriage. At that point he began to see that we had accumulated some material security. We owned the school and had bought other property. He wanted to sell the school for the money. He began fixating about becoming a millionaire.

I finally left him. I got a small apartment for myself and he bought himself a little house in Desert Hot Springs. We tried to keep it civilized. A few months after we separated, we tried to patch the marriage up. We went to counseling. We took a trip to New Zealand and Australia for two months, but he spent most of the time drinking and dowsing (looking for coins and other metals with a dowsing rod). It was a difficult trip for me.

When we came home from the trip, my desire to save the marriage was pretty much over. Jake moved to the desert full time but we stayed in touch. He owned half the school so I knew he had income.

He met some gal at the bar. She got him to buy her a new truck and then she disappeared. He started using marijuana and drinking hard liquor. I don't know what other drugs he took. He ended up becoming extremely paranoid to the point that he put tinfoil on all the windows because he was convinced that the FBI was looking for him. He couldn't keep up payments on the mortgage and lost his house. A couple of times the children and I called the police because we were worried about his safety, but he would convince the police that he was OK.

When my husband died, he was alone. The landlord found him after he had been dead for more than a week in his tiny hovel of an apartment.

Our Thoughts

Jake was a bully. His wife, Diana, was conciliatory. He was emotionally abusive, unbalanced, a philanderer and alcoholic. She was a resilient woman who built a business, dealt with a mentally unstable husband and essentially raised three children on her own. In spite of the fact that Diana was the one who ran the school and had the business savvy to invest in other properties, she did so in a time when women weren't granted the same rights to ownership as they are today. (It wasn't until the 1970s that women in the U.S. were able to have a credit card in their own name.) Jake's erratic behavior, womanizing and drinking put the school's reputation in constant jeopardy. Diana needed to present the school as a safe environment for her young charges and keep the family turmoil a deeply hidden secret. Under those circumstances, it would have been extremely challenging for her to have divorced Jake and kept the business intact.

There were other, complicated reasons that she didn't leave him earlier, too. She knew that Jake did love his children. He might have been demanding of them and in many ways not a great role model, but he taught them skills and a good work ethic. And, as much as he hurt and disappointed her over the years, she was still able to see in him the young firebrand; the compelling ideological champion that he had been when they first met. After he was diagnosed as manic depressive, she excused much of his poor treatment of her and others as a byproduct of his mental illness.

The same passion and commitment Diana applies to the many causes she is involved with today is a reflection of how she fought to keep her marriage together back then.

Diana tried to keep her children shielded from Jake's drinking and bizarre behavior, even into their adult years. One of her sons developed a severe drinking problem in middle age, but the other two children live stable lives, so hard to say if it would have made a difference had Diana separated from Jake while the kids were young.

Alcoholism was only one among many problems, but that does not minimize the damage that Jake's drinking did. People who drink excessively are prone to say and do hurtful, inappropriate things that they wouldn't have said or done if they had been sober. And, while mental health services were minimal, Jake did not take advantage of what was available. If fact, there is no evidence that he made an effort to be a better man, to control his drinking or modify his behavior in any way. And we all know that you cannot change a person who does not want to change.

If we knew someone today who was in a situation similar to Diana's, we would urge them to get the heck out of such a dysfunctional marriage in a hurry; get herself and the kids into counseling, and hire a good public relations firm if necessary to head off damage to the reputation of the school. While counseling and the improved medical resources now available may not save a marriage like this, we cannot see a couple successfully navigating this complex a situation without outside expert advice. For many of us, it can be difficult to give ourselves permission to prioritize our own wellbeing, even when we understand intellectually that we cannot help the other person. But sometimes the only recourse available is to walk away.

I CHOOSE
Kimberly's Story

When Kimberly had unbidden thoughts about her husband dying as the only means of escape from the constant worry from his days-long disappearances when he was drinking, she realized that she needed to retake control of her own life.

※

My relationship with my husband is not well. He has started drinking again. His addiction is back, though, perhaps, it never left us.

"I feel my soul is dying", I texted my husband, "I need to move back to the mountains, to Montana". He made this happen. Less than a year later, a property, a stunning place that we had found online and dreamed about for over three years, became ours. We were ecstatic!

We soon found the home was by far much less stunning than the property itself; it had been abandoned for nearly eight years. Much like people, houses don't like lack of care and abandonment. Water poured from ceiling fixtures. Walls and ceilings were removed due to moisture damage, which also meant removing insulation. I looked at two-by-four studs on the exterior walls, roof trusses and the underside of the metal roofing for six months. This was in the middle of nowhere, where winter winds blast through mountain passes and blizzards last for days at a time.

Additionally, this was the first time either of us 'city-kids' had experienced what it means to live "off-grid". We are afraid to start the diesel generator because it is a big unknown. (Despite what Jerry Seinfeld says, the "unknown" tops the fear list over dying and public speaking.) However, the generator is the only way to run the well and thus, to have water to utilize the indoor facilities. This makes my home on the hill the equivalent of the Hilton, I'm told.

My husband decides the move; the demolition, the remodel and learning to live off-grid aren't enough changes and says, "We need a dog." I love animals and don't say no. We adopt an 80-pound, pure white husky malamute; Ms. Pearl, the first and likely only dog I will ever care for in my adult life. Two months later, I find this precious being on the side of the road in shock, covered in mud and blood. I thought that a car had hit her; later I find out Pearl was actually shot by a neighbor despite absolutely no aggressive behavior on her part. I felt outrageous guilt and burst into action to save her life. This heroic measure cost thousands of dollars and up to four hours a day in additional care for 12 long weeks; time and money that should have gone into winterizing the house and creating a very large pile of firewood for heat in preparation for the cold months ahead.

I am tired. I am stressed. My neighbor Jim, who utilizes the private road through our property to reach his even more remote cabin, visits me at work. He hands me my husband's phone, which looks as though it has been run over; says he found it by the gate of the property's private road. My face goes pale. I know immediately and intuitively what this means. I try to play it off for my neighbor's sake and to avoid probing questions in public.

My husband is on another bender. I don't know where he is. I'm worried that he's passed out somewhere... and even if he does become lucid, there is now no way to contact him or vice versa because his phone is in my hands, broken. He's already been gone for more than a day. Every muscle tenses. I have shortness of breath. I'm on the verge of tears every moment. I imagine the worst. I imagine he is wrapped around a tree. I admit to myself that, though it will shatter my heart into a thousand more pieces, I hope this time he dies from driving drunk. Then and only then, will his family and I be saved from this constant worry of "What next?"

I call my sister in hysterics and am finally able to release an ocean of tears. She listens supportively and then says, "You're my big sister. I've always looked up to you. You're the strongest person I know. If ANYONE can do this, YOU CAN." I tearfully respond, "But I don't want to be strong anymore."

My husband returns home several days later. He finds me in the backyard sitting quietly in a chair looking at some of the most majestic landscape in all of North America. He looks haggard and remorseful, though I don't remember an apology ever spoken. If there was or had been, I wouldn't have believed it anyway because he still seems half drunk. I look at him with as much compassion as I can muster and say, "I need a different reality. I don't want to be married to you anymore. I told you four years ago when you came home filthy from being falling down drunk on the streets I couldn't be married to a disgusting drunk and to someone I couldn't respect. I begged you then to do something about this issue. I've prayed over you for hours at a time, waiting for you to awaken from the blackness. You chose to follow a program for less than a month. You were blacked out drunk, belligerent and paranoid for our fifth wedding anniversary. You didn't even attempt anything to heal the root causes of this disease, outside a session with a life coach, a couple of AA meetings and a couple of sessions with a healer. You obviously want to continue your affair with alcohol more than you want to have a wife."

He knows he has lost his self-proclaimed "soul-mate." I have put a stake in the ground. Though devastated, I finally remembered my power of choice.

I have learned that I have the power of choice in every moment of every day. I choose to have a new reality, one without a person who chooses to stay unhealthy. I choose to have healthy boundaries and to practice self-care.

Our Thoughts

In Alcoholic's Anonymous they call it a "Geographic:" moving to a new location to have a fresh start. When we are unhappy, we sometimes idealize change. As they say, wherever you go, there you are.

Kimberly's wish, her belief, that this move would help her husband stop drinking and bring them closer blinded her to harsh realities that a more objective perspective would have uncovered. So here they were, off the grid, out of their element and in over their heads. Even without the alcoholism, this would have been a challenging situation for most couples.

They were financially committed to the fixer-upper. There was ego involved. No one likes to admit they have made a mistake or to be seen as a quitter. She had already invested ten years in their relationship. She had to endure intense psychological and spiritual pain before she was able to admit that he wasn't going to be the man she needed him to be.

Why had Kimberly and her husband left Montana the first time and why did they believe that going back would be better this time? Her husband had been binge drinking and disappearing for days on end periodically for years. He had not sought help to deal with his drinking.

We are relieved that she ultimately chose to focus on her own health and wellbeing. It is sad that she had to endure such prolonged pain to get to that place, but we well understand that she needed to feel that she had exhausted all possible efforts to help her husband overcome his alcoholism and to hold on to her marriage.

MAKING GOOD ON SECOND CHANCES
Janet's Story

Just as choosing to cut ties with the alcoholic is a wrenching choice, so sometimes is the decision to stay, especially when you have been repeatedly deceived, as was the case with this wife. Commitment, boundaries and a broad circle of support by family, friends and professionals made sobriety a reality in this husband's life.

My husband Connor was a heavy drinker in college, but then all of our friends drank during those years, too, and so he didn't really stand out. If I were to be completely honest with myself, there were signs all along that he had a problem. At parties I would count his drinks sometimes. I remember finding an empty bottle once in his backpack. He always had a rationale for his drinking, though, and he seemed fine.

Then he got a DUI. He called me from the police department. He'd been on his way home and was literally a block away from our house when he got pulled over. I remember him calling from the police department and just spilling, "I'm an alcoholic. I have a problem."

Connor quit drinking following the arrest. At that time, we'd been together for eleven years. He went to one or two AA meetings and I went to one or two Al Anon meetings. He decided that AA wasn't for him. Alcoholics are fabulous rationalizers and he's among the best. He was a scientist. He didn't believe in God. He didn't buy in to the whole higher power thing.

He seemed to do great for long time. He taught classes and seemed to be the model citizen. After the DUI incident we celebrated Connor's sober anniversary every year. But while we were celebrating his sobriety, he was secretly drinking.

He still doesn't remember when it happened, when he first started drinking again. He doesn't recall there being a trigger. I remember many nights when he seemed a little off balance. I would ask him, "You're acting really weird. Are you drinking again? Are you on something?" I know some people fall off the wagon. People drink again. People relapse. He had always promised me that if that ever happened, he would tell me. Looking back, obviously at some level, I knew, even though I never found bottles. He was really good at hiding his drinking.

As is common with heavy drinkers, Connor built up a tolerance, but then his body couldn't handle it anymore and he got scared. He thought he was dying. He didn't know how to get from "I'm scared" to "I'll stop." I came to hate Sundays because every Sunday he was grumpy. He'd tell me it was because he was behind on work. I didn't realize that he would try not to drink while he was home on the weekends. And by Sunday he was really jonesin' for his booze.

One especially bad night eight years ago, which was around what I thought to be his anniversary of seven year's sober – I feel so dumb when I think about it – Connor had been sick for a several days. He said that had the stomach flu. Well, I know now that he was trying to detox himself. He was finally feeling better and was working late. I was anxiously waiting for Connor to get home when I got a call from his dad. Connor was drunk and he thought he was dying and needed someone to come pick him up. (He had called his mom, which still irritates the living hell out of me, that he didn't call me.) Thank God for my father-in-law because he insisted on letting me know what was going on before she did anything. He went with me when I took Connor to the hospital.

Connor was fine. He was not dying. His liver was not failing. But the doctor told him, given his blood alcohol level - .35, and he wasn't even slurring his words, it was clear he had a "pretty serious drinking problem." He thought his toes were turning yellow. He thought he had killed his liver. Sitting in the waiting room with him, I was so mad. And all I could smell was the booze. I couldn't believe it. We had talked about it and he had promised me. Connor couldn't remember how long he'd been drinking again. I knew that night that it had been a long time because he was so far gone. The doctor recommended that my husband go to rehab.

I left him at the hospital and went home to get a few hours of sleep. My head was spinning. The doctor had said Connor could detox at home, but people die when detoxing. It's not common but it can happen. All I was thinking was that I have a four year old; I've got to get my husband out of the house. I found a place and by that afternoon he was in an in-patient rehab facility.

My insurance agency told me at the time – this still pisses me off – they would cover detox but not rehab. But I knew it was life and death so I put it on my credit card. We had to suck it up if I wanted him to live. We would deal with the money later.

There was so much guilt and shame. Connor didn't want to be in our town so I took him to a treatment center about 30 miles south. It was a really basic place — they got bed bugs at one point — and he was there with felons that could bypass jail by going to rehab instead. But my whole thing was, "you screwed up. This is not a vacation. And you're there to work."

The center ended up being great. It was a thirty-day program. He had a fabulous counselor. Many counselors had been there in recovery themselves. Saturday's were family day and I did the whole thing kicking and screaming. I was so resentful. I remember the first time I spoke at an Al Anon meeting I told them they all seemed to like being there, which of course they all laughed at because none of us wanted to be there. It just made me so angry, but I went because I knew that no matter what Connor did with his life, I had to be in a good place because I had a son to raise.

I went to several meetings in the area, and ended up finding one I really liked, on Monday mornings while my son was in preschool. It was primarily women. I went there until I was ready to deliver our second son, two years later.

Right before my husband's 30 days was up, I was scared. I still had a lot of anger and I wasn't ready for him to come home. I talked to his counselor and she said he wasn't ready either. "If you can swing it, I really recommend another thirty days."

One month of rehab was ridiculously expensive, like $7,000. I told my boss at the time, a recovering alcoholic himself, what was going on and, incredibly, he offered to pay for that second month.

I took our son to see his father once. He didn't know what was happening except that his Daddy was gone and Daddy, even when drinking, had been a fabulous, present dad – as much as a person who is drinking can be.

I had a really frank conversation with my husband's counselor, and he recommended that we lay it all on the line. I knew that I wasn't going to go through another relapse with him again. I'd been through it twice. I wasn't going to put my kid through that again. The counselor helped me have this straightforward conversation with him. It wasn't a threat. It wasn't an ultimatum. It was just my reality. You could see his whole attitude change. I said, "It's totally up to you if you want to come home now and try it, we can do that. But this is it." And he chose – he chose to stay 30 days. I don't think he would be here today if he had only done the first 30 days.

The second thirty days he just seemed to get it and he put his all into it. I was still scared when he came home, but he was obviously different. He's been all in — hook, line and sinker with AA ever since. He's had two sponsors and he has sponsored three others and still goes to meetings and enjoys them. His department at work was fabulous. He was gone the better part of a semester. They actually called in a drug and alcohol counselor to one of their staff meetings to answer their questions about alcoholism and what my husband might be like when he came back and how they could welcome him. They sent us gift cards for food and such while he was in rehab just to help my son and me out. For as hard as it was to be a single parent for 60 days, I had so much love and support.

My mother-in-law, who had a long history of self-medicating with alcohol, got sober after my husband's ordeal. She is still doing great. She and my father-in-law have gone back to church and bible study, and they both go to one, if not two, meetings a week. At first she was one of those people who, when she did go to meetings, sat in the back and never talked. Now she has taken on commitments at the meetings. It has really changed the whole family.

My own family welcomed my husband back with open arms. My mom did have a blunt conversation with Connor. She said, "I love you and support you, but you do this to my daughter and grandson again and I'm going to have to kill you." She said it lightly, but they both understood how she felt.

There are a lot of good reasons that this time around Connor has been able to stay sober. He found a support group. He had support from his family and his friends from work. I explained the reality of what he was going to lose and that helped him really get serious about recovery. Now he says he sees it every day: he would never risk losing his kids and me. That knowledge keeps him motivated and going meetings.

We talked about the "Little Box" in Al Anon. That place for thoughts that you are not ready or willing to deal with right now, but have tucked away for a time when you are ready to face it. Connor obviously drove while impaired with our son in the car. That's what I've set aside - it's just too scary to deal with. I don't know if we'll ever be able to discuss that. And at this point, it's not worth getting angry over. It's done now. Nobody ever got hurt.

We've been quite open with our older son although our younger son is too small to understand. My husband used to go to an AA meeting in a park downtown on Saturday mornings and so he took our older son to those meetings a lot. The men sat in a circle and the playground was right there and they'd all kind of watch him play while they had their meeting. We've been open with him about how Daddy's an alcoholic and what that means and the family connection to it.

When my family drinks our son sees normal alcohol use and we talk about unhealthy alcohol use. We talk about sobriety and AA. We try to make it kind of normal — showing our son that some people drink and it's fine for them, but it's not OK for others.

A lot of times people do want to stop drinking, but they don't change their environment so they get sucked back in. That may be one of the benefits of being a closet drinker. We partied with friends a lot, but my husband drank all by himself so he didn't have to change his social group like so many addicts do. We try to be grateful for these things.

This gratitude has really helped with his recovery. Both of us really try to be grateful. It's a huge part of staying positive. Getting out of self helps, too. Being of service helps. That's why he takes on these sponsees.

We are pretty open at this point. I'm sure there is stuff we haven't covered. We discuss things as they come up. It's his story so I ask him before I share his story.

Our Thoughts

In the previous story, Kimberly gave her husband repeated chances to change as did Janet in this story. So why is this a success story and Kimberly's was not? The obvious difference is that Connor not only acknowledged his drinking problem but also made – and continues to make – a sincere and diligent effort to maintain his sobriety by attending AA meetings on a regular basis, working with a sponsor, and working the 12-step program. He is well aware of all that he stands to lose if he starts drinking again: his wife and children, his career, and the esteem of his colleagues and professional community.

It took fear for his life, a firm stand from his wife and a second consecutive 30-day turn at a rehab facility to be in a mental state where he could think rationally about his life and decide that he wanted to hold on to his family and become truly sober. He was able to overcome the shame, humiliation, and guilt of having deceived and betrayed his wife, his children, and his co-workers by facing up to what he had become and the pain he had caused others. Every day he shows them through his words and actions that he is serious about being sober and earning their respect.

For her part, Janet attended Al-anon meetings (albeit with a grain of resentment), went to joint counseling with Connor, and was willing to speak openly and candidly about her feelings. She sheltered her children, as best she could, from the fallout of Connor's drinking and shouldered a greater burden of their care while Connor was getting sober.

It has been a number of years now since Connor stopped drinking, but there are still moments when Janet can't shake the feeling that the other shoe could drop any minute. She has forgiven, but may never be able to fully let down her guard against the possibility of him drinking again. She is well aware of how powerful a hold alcohol can have on a person with an addictive personality.

HIDDEN BOTTLES
Bob's Story

Split personality traits are a hallmark of many drinkers. Did the drinking change this wife's personality, or was it that the spigot of repressed emotions, opened by the alcohol, released anger in equal proportion to the amount of wine consumed?

I was at a low point in my life when I first met Sheila; I'd lost my job and everything in my life was falling apart. She had a daughter who was eight-years-old and one who was seventeen. She seemed to have her life under control. And she was so supportive and understanding. A few months after we started dating Sheila suggested I rent out my house and move in with her. I thought about it and, a month later when I hadn't found another job yet, that's what I did.

It wasn't long after I moved in with her that I discovered that Sheila had an alcohol problem. She covered it up really well at first and it took a while for me to catch on. When we had first started dating, we would go out to dinner, go to movies, all the usual things couples do, but after just a few weeks of living together, Sheila began wanting to spend evenings in just watching TV. She would avoid having to go out. One time we were driving to a movie and halfway there she said that she didn't feel well, that she wanted to go home. She even said she was claustrophobic in theaters. I realized later that it was because she wanted to go home to drink.

Her personality changed when she had more than a glass or two of wine. It was like she transitioned into being another person. She went from kind and generous to angry. She would say and do things that were hurtful.

IN THE DRINK

I talked to her about her drinking. She told me that she started drinking when her first husband got sick with leukemia and passed away. She was just 22 years old and he was 54. She had another husband before me and he did a number on her. She said her second husband tried to kill her with drugs, but I think he was misguidedly trying to treat her for bipolar disorder with lithium. He wasn't a medical professional; he was a Catholic priest who became an Episcopalian priest in order to marry her. It was pretty weird.

I felt like none of this excused how she lashed out at the girls when she was drunk. She could be verbally abusive to her daughters, calling them bitches and whores. The way she talked to her kids, it was painful to hear. Did she really feel that way about her beautiful daughters? The girls pretty much blew her off like this wasn't new to them. They mostly just left the room, but I could see the hurt.

After high school graduation, the older daughter moved out to live with friends and I realized that I didn't want her youngest daughter – this wonderful, sweet, beautiful, little eight-year-old – being raised all alone by an alcoholic. I made a commitment to myself that I'd see her through college.

I found a job about 100 miles from where we lived. Sheila helped me buy a recreational vehicle which we moved near the job for me to live in. Then Sheila decided to sell her house and move in with me. I probably should have said at that point, "No. Don't do that. I don't see us having a future." But I didn't and we wound up buying a house together. The night before we were going to move into our new home, we stayed in the trailer. Something set her off, she was just screaming and going crazy I said, "Honey, calm down. We've got people right next door." In the middle of the night, she grabbed her daughter and left. I don't know where she went. She showed up in time to get the keys to the new house, though. That was a bad night.

When she was drunk, Sheila would act out in mean, unpredictable ways. My new job had me getting up at 5 a.m., so I'd try to go to bed at 10 p.m., and she was just getting started at 10. She'd come up to the bedroom at 11:30 or so really angry and want to talk. I'd try to fake sleep. She'd wind up smacking me in the back of the head, trying to wake me up.

She had to quit her job to move in with me and I told her that there was no need for her to get a new job. I was making good money. But Sheila said that she needed to work to save herself. To my amazement, she opened up the paper, saw an ad, went down to the local city hall, applied, and a few weeks later she got the job. It was a really good position with career potential. Sheila was a highly functional alcoholic who could be quite personable. She could be rip snorting drunk one night and the next morning could get up and act like nothing happened. I really never saw her hung over.

I don't think she drank at work, but she would every evening. I'd say to her, "Why don't you put the bottle in the cabinet, sit down and have a glass with me? I know that you're drinking so what's the use of hiding it? Maybe you won't feel so angry about having to do it that way." She never did. She'd go upstairs where I'm sure she guzzled right out of the bottle. She never came back downstairs with a glass of wine. She had bottles hidden everywhere; in closets, in the garage. Mostly, it was the $10 a gallon cheap stuff.

One Christmas we had my kids from my previous marriage over and Sheila slapped me hard right in front of them. Her mood had changed from happy hostess to angry drunk without warning. I tried to downplay it in front of my kids, but they remembered it. They didn't like her for that.

There were other times, though, when she could be generous and kind. A few years later when my son needed $5,000 and I didn't have that much to give to him, Sheila gave me the rest of it. She had also sold her house to be with me, so I felt kind of obligated for those reasons. That's why I eventually married her. Also, I didn't want her daughter growing up seeing her mom living with a guy she wasn't married to. Part of the reason that it took me three years to marry her was that I tried to hang sobriety over her head as a condition. Stop drinking and we'll get married. It didn't work, though, and eventually her daughter's well being was more important to me than Sheila not drinking.

Sheila's drinking habits stayed pretty much the same through the ten years that we were together, although there were peaks where she seemed more angry. When she was drinking, she seemed to want to hurt somebody or even get hurt. She fell down the stairs once. Another time she was drunk and fell and broke her arm. And there was the time she fell and split her lip. There was blood everywhere. Her face looked bad for a week. I was so afraid that she'd call the police and say, "He beat me" and I'd wind up going to jail because that's the way it is. She could be mean enough to do that. I didn't want to be involved in it anymore. It was just too toxic. But I had made a pact with myself that I would take care of her daughter and so I stuck it out.

I had an employee assistance program at work so two times we went to a counselor. At one point, Sheila said, "My husband doesn't listen to me. He doesn't take me seriously."

The counselor already had a pretty good grasp of what was going on. The counselor said, "I'm sorry, but no one takes an alcoholic seriously." So, of course, we never went back to her.

We went to another therapist a couple of years later, a male this time. The whole purpose of us going there was to discuss our life with her drinking. Sheila would bring up stuff that was just off the wall. She saw a picture of a girl in a bathing suit on my phone and she said that I looked at porn. The problem that we came for no longer was the issue that the therapist took to heart. It seemed to me that he was attracted to her and it changed his whole focus. He called her at home one night, saying he was concerned and asking if she was OK, if everything was all right. Even Sheila got creeped out. We never went back to him after that.

She went to an AA meeting one time. Afterwards she said, "This isn't for me." They had some hardcore people there who were living under stairwells and stuff like that. I tried a lot of times to get involved in Al-Anon. The meetings were not convenient or regular. Sometimes only a couple of people would show up. It wasn't an effective tool for me.

My hope was always that she would get her life together. I had a good job and was making good money. She had a great job. We were OK financially and had a nice house. I had hoped that all of that combined would be enough incentive for her to stop drinking.

I left her a number of times while we were married. I'd take my dog and go to a motel. I'd spend a week there and she'd beg me to come back. She'd promise, "I'm going to stop drinking. I'll get help."

Nothing ever held up. In fact, one time I told her I wanted her to set up a $5,000 savings account for me so that I could have first and last month's rent for a place and move out if she kept drinking. "Oh, yeah. We can do that," she'd said. We never did. It just came to a point when I said, "enough" and left.

Even with the terrible things she said to her daughters, the years of her verbal abuse, when it came time for me to leave Sheila they both stood by their mother's side. To this day they don't talk to me. I didn't really expect anything from the older daughter, but I thought that the younger one who I helped raise would have recognized and appreciated my effort.

I met with Sheila a few times after the separation to talk. One time I met her at a coffee shop at her request. She made all of those promises again, told me she needed to have me back. I just unloaded on her. I told her, "You have been a terrible wife. You drank. You slapped me in front of my own children." I reminded her of all these things and it's like it all just went over her head. She just went back to the same, "We need to get back together before it's too late." But for me, it was already too late. I filed for divorce five months after I left her that last time.

Sheila had the job with the city for ten years. She lost it when we were going through the divorce. I know that she didn't like her boss; she may have been inebriated enough to speak her mind, something of that nature. I don't know what the situation was. I had to give her $1,800 a month.

The younger daughter, Daniela, is an adult now. She's gotten her master's degree and works at the university. She got married and has a baby. She seems to be doing all right. She's the silver lining for the years I was with Sheila. I ran into Sheila when she had the baby with her. Sheila said that she watches the baby for her daughter all the time. She's even converted her daughter's old bedroom into a nursery. I find it pretty interesting that Daniela would have enough confidence in her mother, knowing that she's an alcoholic, to allow her to watch her baby. But I did notice some physical differences in Sheila. She didn't have that same look of the alcoholic. She had gained weight but no longer had the potbelly that drinkers get.

I don't have any regrets for having married Sheila. If I had any influence on Daniela's life, that's all I need. With that in mind, I have no regrets. I wish it had been different but nothing is a fairy book story.

I met a wonderful woman and am now happily married to her. I believe Sheila has someone special in her life now, too. If my leaving woke her up, then that's great. I hope that my leaving her had a positive impact on her life.

Our Thoughts

Bob, the husband, was "at a low point" when he first met Sheila and so emotionally vulnerable at that time that he didn't see beyond her kindnesses to him. His first impression was that she seemed financially stable and was a good mother to her daughters. By the time he recognized the depth of her flaws — the drinking, anti-social tendencies, and the history of her curious, if not totally bizarre, previous marriages — Bob had already bonded with and felt responsible for the younger daughter and no longer trusted Shelia to be a dependable parent. In short order, their roles reversed, with Bob becoming the stable one, and Shelia becoming almost childlike with her self-centeredness, temper tantrums, and rash decision-making.

He made an attempt to leave her once, using a job offer out of the area as an excuse to separate, but couldn't muster the resolve to make a clean break when she decided to move with him. The drinking and tantrums accelerated. She began being physically abusive to him. Bob talked a lot about staying with her out of a sense of duty to the younger daughter. He thought that he could help Shelia who he came to believe had mental health issues. He was also exhibiting classic signs of both emotional and physical domestic abuse. Looking at their relationship through that lens, it is no wonder that it took so long for him to extricate himself from this unhappy marriage. Even after Bob landed a good job with a substantial paycheck, he continued to carry with him the insecurities of the down years. His faltering confidence in himself was amplified by Shelia's ill treatment and belittling of him.

Bob took the right step in insisting upon marriage counseling. It is unfortunate that the first therapist took a tact that put Shelia on the defensive. We all close ourselves off when we feel that we are under attack. A trained therapist should have known better. After the creepy and highly unethical behavior of the second therapist, it is no surprise that they abandoned that avenue.

Bob finally broke away from this dysfunctional alcoholic a few years ago, although it was hard on his wallet to do so. He has had the opportunity to say his piece to her, to confront her with his truth about her. Now he expresses only good will toward his ex-wife. He is happy to see the daughter grown and takes pride in the role he played in helping her along the way. He has a pragmatic outlook and new love in his life today. He says he has "no regrets." That concept may be the magic ingredient that helped him find peace and happiness.

Children
of a drinking parent

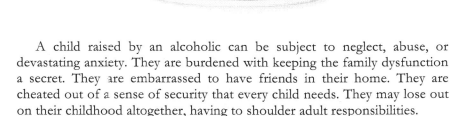

A child raised by an alcoholic can be subject to neglect, abuse, or devastating anxiety. They are burdened with keeping the family dysfunction a secret. They are embarrassed to have friends in their home. They are cheated out of a sense of security that every child needs. They may lose out on their childhood altogether, having to shoulder adult responsibilities.

They develop emotional walls to protect themselves from disappointment and hurt. They may act out and become self-destructive, turning to alcohol themselves. Or they may run to the other extreme, seeking out love wherever they can find it. Low self-esteem and a belief that they aren't worthy of love can lead to bad choices in where they seek comfort.

These children need to understand that it is not their fault that their parent is an alcoholic. It is not their responsibility to take care of their parent or to keep the drinking a secret. What they need most is a sober, caring, responsible adult that they can turn to for reassurance, guidance and perhaps intervention.

If you survived growing up with an alcoholic parent, congratulations! Now that you are an adult, make wise choices for yourself and your own future. Let go of as much of the anger, disappointment and hurt as you can, and build yourself a good life. You cannot let your dysfunctional parent's problems be your responsibility, but you can take care of yourself.

LIKE FATHER, LIKE SON?
Irene's Story

The imprint of a dominant personality in the intimate family environment has a profound effect on adolescents. When that person is an abusive drunk, the cycle of abuse, drinking and domination is too often carried over to the next generation. This is the story of how one father's example paved the way for his son's drinking and self-destructive choices.

ROGER

I grew up in the petite mid-western town of Chicago Heights, Illinois; tucked out of sight an hour-plus south of Chicago, a place commonly referred to by Dan the Weatherman on ABC Channel 7 as the "boonies." In the 60's when I was just a pup, our town was mostly blue-collar workers with union jobs at the sprawling plants owned by Ford, U.S. Steel, Kimball Glass, Victor Chemical and Jay's Potato Chips.

My father, Roger Henry, stuck out in our ethnically diverse neighborhood of Hispanics and Blacks, Polish and Italians as he was German and Irish, six-foot even, a slender pale man with a solid mop of blonde hair that was always whisked back in the front to portray his deep sapphire eyes. Roger was the only male child to carry on the Henry family name. He had three sisters; our Aunts Phyllis, Chutzy (never knew her real name) and Ann (the nicest of all).

My mother, Mary Guadalupe Henry, stood in stark contrast to my dad. She was an even five foot, carried the burnt bronze Spanish/Italian skin tones and the thick, wavy, jet black Sophia Loren hair. Her eyes, dark chocolate orbs, were all-seeing and could stop any of her four kids in their tracks without muttering a word. We knew that stare meant whatever antic we were thinking of was not to happen.

We had recently moved into our grandparent's 1½ story shingled home, complete with an attic window over the sun porch roof and a full, unfinished basement. Unbeknownst to us children at the time, Dad had lost our home in Steger to some gambling tryst at the racetrack.

On what began as a typical sizzling hot summer day with a layer of relentless, sticky humidity, we four kids – my older brother Patrick (ten), me (eight), Michael (six) and our youngest sister, Rose Ann (four) — were playing outside when we saw what was becoming a common occurrence: our Dad arriving home in the middle of a work week day.

As we ran through the back door into the kitchen we could hear my Dad asking Mom for lunch whilst he settled himself in the pine green high-backed chair. Patrick made a PB&J sandwich for Michael and Rose Ann while Mom prepared Dad's favorite — a pickle peanut butter sandwich with a scoop of cottage cheese on the side — and then asked that I bring the plate to "my father."

Dad sat with his back to us. The late lunch hour had placed the sun just so; its rays were sent splicing through the living room's stained glass side window, causing the sunrays to dance with reds, yellow and greens across the darkened, well-worn wooden floor. A flowered metal TV stand stood to the side of the chair, the TV blaring some adult nonsense loudly. Father was making snoring-like noises, the scent of stale beer cloaked all about.

With fear as my guide, so as not to disturb Dad, I gently placed the china plate on the tray; nonetheless, the dink of china to metal woke him from his semi-slumber. He was immediately angry. "Irene is this all there is for lunch? This is crap. Go ask your mother for something better, meat," he barked.

Dad threw the plate through the air; it landed upside down between the living room and kitchen entryway, dotting the dark wooden floor and the kitchen's grey speckled linoleum with cottage cheese.

Dad stalked over to Mom and grabbed her arm, yanked her to her knees. "Clean this mess up and bring me food. Now!"

Pat, Michael and I ran to Mom as Dad smacked her hard to the floor. "Roger, this is all we have. Really it is."

Mom was on her knees picking up the bits of cottage cheese when Dad took a step towards her, reached down, grabbed a fistful of Mom's hair, jerked her to her feet like a rag doll and dragged her into the living room.

We all four encircled Mom, trying to pull her away from Dad in a sick game of tug of war. Dad turned around and slammed Mom's back into the arm of the chair, raised his fist high in the air and thrust one punch solidly into Mom's chest. As Dad raised his fist a second time, six-year-old Michael got in between them, taking the main thrust of Dad's punch right into the side of his head.

Michael's head fell flat on mom's chest; he was stunned by the blow. Mom bent over Michael, forming a shield. Patrick jumped up on Dad's back, circling his neck with his arms to pull Dad down. I grabbed Dad's belt with both of my hands, pulling, acting as an anchor, anything to separate Dad from Mom and Michael.

Dad grabbed Patrick by the arm and flicked him off as if he was an annoying flea. I released my hold on Dad's belt and we both dashed to cover Mom where she was bent over crying. Poor Michael was still dazed.

Our parents separated. We moved out of our grandparent's home and moved into the first-floor unit in a two-story home. One front door served as the main entry to the home that was split by a common hallway. A stairwell led upstairs to Mrs. Russo's (our landlady's mother) apartment.

Mom and Dad patched things up, but the drinking and abuse soon returned. After one more brief separation and reconciliation, one more drunken beating, more weeks of little or no food as the meager earnings went to replenish Father's alcohol or gambling fix, Mom and Dad divorced.

The day Mom served Dad with the divorce papers was quite epic through the eyes of this eight year old. Generally on a Friday night, Mom worked at restaurant events and was not home 'till midnight. Dad normally arrived any time after 6:00 p.m., usually drunk. But on that Friday, Mom was home waiting for us after school. She asked us all to sit with her at the kitchen table.

"I have something to tell you. Your dad and I are going to get a divorce, the divorce papers are sitting on the bannister in the front hallway where he will see them first thing when he gets home tonight. Your Dad is not allowed in our home any longer. I can no longer take the chance that one of you will be hurt. Your dad is a good man and loves you all very much. It is the alcohol he cannot give up."

The Knife

We heard when Dad entered the main hallway. We all stood frozen in place on the opposite side of our apartment's door, staring at the doorknob. Dad turned the knob back and forth only to find it was locked. Mom shooed us off, then told Dad through the door: "Roger you need to read the letter on the stairwell bannister."

There was quiet. Then we heard the sound of creaking wooden floorboards, paper tearing, another stretch of quiet and then yelling and cursing. Dad pounded and kicked on our door, threatening to kill us, himself, Mom and whomever else he could name on Mom's side of the family. He said that if Mom even thought that she, the "dumb Mexican," was going to divorce him, she was crazy.

Round, rosy-cheeked Mrs. Russo, five feet tall and 250 pounds, hurried halfway down the stairs, gripping a wooden baseball bat, and ordered my dad to leave. She had already called the police and they were on their way.

Dad left before the police arrived and the tension eased. At last, we all had what we needed most. Peace. Patrick and Michael fell asleep in their double bed, a hospital hand-me-down. Mom, Rose Ann and I were soundly sleeping on the matching bed on the opposite side of the room.

We were startled out of our collective deep sleep when a throaty voice yelled out: "I will kill you myself Mary if you don't say you will take me back, right now." Dad was standing over our bed, knife in hand.

The vivid memory of that moment haunts me to this day. Mom bolted upright in bed and screamed, "Roger don't!" We kids all started crying and screaming, too. A sliver of streetlight piercing the darkness was the room's only illumination. The familiar acrid smell of sweat and booze filled the air. Mom, pulling us in beside her, demanded, pleaded that we children be quiet.

Mrs. Russo appeared at our front door, breathless, "Mary I called the police and they are on their way. Roger, I have this bat and I will crack your head wide open if you hurt anyone." We could now see the patrol car lights out front, sending intermittent bursts of red light through our bedroom. The police had a bright white spotlight beaming on our front door.

Relief, the police were here, no one would die tonight. The police took Dad away and told him that he could come back tomorrow and get his clothes.

Aunt Irene, Uncle Tommy (who was a police officer) and Grandpa came for us. That night and for the next three nights all five of us slept in the same bed at Grandma's.

Sometime after "Dad's freak-out," and on too many occasions to recall, I would have a reoccurring nightmare where Dad murdered Mom that evening and from a dead sleep I would sit straight up in bed screaming and calling out "Mom, Mom, Mom!" until she would finally answer me. For me to find peace and return to sleep I had to hear Mom's voice to make sure she was still alive. I armed myself with a knife that I kept hidden between my mattress and box spring.

During my high school freshman year, the family rumor tree said my father had moved to Florida. For the first time since I was ten years old I slept peacefully; no knife, no nightmares. It was good to go to sleep without fear.

The emotional scars of our father's abuse and subsequent abandonment stayed with us long after we lost contact with him, though. My older brother Patrick was so reluctant to take on the role of male head of our household that he fled to seminary boarding school.

Rose Ann's first husband drank himself to sleep most nights and beat her on more than one occasion. Without a father around, exposed at an early age to Mom being verbally and physically abused left my sister lost, with no backbone and not believing in herself. It took several years of abuse, the birth of her second child and my assistance to get her to exit from the marriage.

I, too, experienced the drunken tirades, the abuse, the lack of food and heat in the winter. But I also saw a strong, determined mom who decided that the four of us children would all stay together and tried her best to provide for us and to bring us up morally grounded and knowing that we were loved. At a young age, I actively decided not to allow someone else's weaknesses, faults, sins, to define me. Long ago, I vowed to never be unprepared, to always have the means to protect my loved ones and myself. My motto is 'victor not victim.'

MICHAEL

As with most families with several children, birth order accounted for differences in how each of us was treated. Both before and after the divorce, Patrick, as the oldest of us kids, was put in charge when our parents weren't home. When something went wrong, he was also the one that got a beating.

After Dad struck Michael who was attempting to shield Mom from a blow, Michael could do no wrong in her eyes. The degree to which she turned a blind eye to Michael's transgressions grew even more pronounced following the divorce.

Everyone in the family was protective of Rose Ann, who was the youngest, and also often sickly in her early childhood. No one really seemed to pay much attention to me. I did what I was told and my occasional harmless escapades went unnoticed, under the radar.

Mom, the family's sole provider after the divorce, started working more hours at the restaurant, leaving us kids to fend for ourselves most afternoons and evenings, although the neighbors provided some oversight, telling us to "Get down out of that tree. You know better!" and things like that. The priests and nuns knew our situation and would often send us home with apples and other treats. I had no idea at the time that those snacks were the discards from other children's lunches.

When Michael was ten years old, he started up with his shenanigans, ditching school and smoking cigarettes in the back yard. After Patrick went off to seminary boarding school the next year, it fell to me to shoulder many of the household responsibilities: things like being there for my younger brother and sister after school, getting dinner made and making sure they got their teeth brushed if Mom wasn't home by bedtime. I did what I could to help out, but Michael never listened to me when I tried to stop him from getting into mischief. I was only two years older than him and really just a kid myself.

By age fourteen, Michael and two friends, Russ and McCoy, who also attended St. Ann's school, not-so-secretly drank beer in the basement. Michael started staying out late. My mom had basically no control over him. At her wits end, she sent him to Glenwood School for Boys. We were told that it was a military school modeled after West Point that taught leadership training. But it was also a place where they sent bad boys who needed discipline. Michael fell in with a couple of boys who had already been in trouble with the law. Shoplifting. Smoking pot. Michael ended up being expelled from Glenwood during his junior year.

Back at home, Michael severely disrupted the calm that had settled over the household during the two years when he had been in boarding school and it had been just Mom, Rose Ann and I in the house. Michael was an ass. He acted like a little dictator, like he was now in charge. When he was at military school, he was required to make his bed every day and do his own laundry, but when he came home he seemed to think that, with three women in the house, he no longer needed to do those things for himself.

He started hanging out with McCoy again. They would come home drunk or high or both. The two went to the Kentucky Fried Chicken drive-through one Friday night, in our dinky, little town where everyone knows which car belongs to whom. There was a gun lying on the front seat between them. Neither of them picked up the gun when they robbed the place, but when they were arrested, they were automatically charged with armed robbery. McCoy, for reasons that are not clear to me, was assigned primary responsibility – maybe he had been the one to come up with the plan and had talked Michael into it. At any rate, Michael did not have to go to jail. No one in the family talked about it even though it was in the local newspaper.

Mom let him stay on at the house and tried to set new rules; Michael could only stay if there was no drinking or pot smoking, he had to go to school and he had to get a job. But Michael just continued on as before, drinking and all the rest of it. Uncle Victor, who was also Michael's godfather, had a lot of heart-to-hearts with him, but Michael wasn't willing to listen to anyone or do anything except what he wanted to do. He stole money, mostly from me, a considerable amount that I had been saving up to go to law school. I confronted him about it, demanding that he return the money several times. He choked me once when I accused him. I still don't want to think about how far he would have gone if McCoy hadn't pulled him off me.

Mom, her siblings and I had many discussions about making Michael move out. We were in agreement that it would be best for everyone, that his drinking and belligerent behavior was getting worse, but it wasn't until the landlord gave us notice — we had to move because he wanted to let his son take over the apartment — that Mom found a reason to get Michael out of our home that she could live with. She rented a smaller apartment and told Michael that there wasn't going to be enough room for him. I could stay because I was going to community college and also helping with the rent.

Michael didn't take it seriously because Mom had always given in to him before. He didn't believe she wouldn't let him come with us. On the day we were packing, he asked Mom for the new address and I butted in, "It doesn't matter because you are not coming."

He turned to Mom and asked, "Are you really throwing your own son out onto the street?" He was trying to shame her into letting him come with us.

To which I replied, "You're not putting this on Mom. She's not putting you on the street. You're doing that to yourself." For once, Mom stuck to her guns.

Diane

Michael ended up living at his girlfriend's parent's house, at first sleeping on the living room couch and then moving into their basement. Michael completely charmed his girlfriend, Diane, and her parents. He was careful to only present his best side to them. They felt sorry for him; thought that his family had treated him horribly.

Michael met Diane while he was still at Glenwood School for Boys. She lived in an affluent suburb of Chicago, some distance from our neighborhood. Transportation issues didn't allow them to see a lot of each other early on, so they didn't really know each other very well at the time he moved in with her family, even though they had been dating for more than two years.

Michael was Diane's first real boyfriend. Her upbringing in Olympia Fields with its large houses, golf course and country club was a stark contrast to the working class town where Michael had grown up. Diane, as teenage girls often are, was attracted to Michael, at least in part, because it was a thrill for her to date a guy with that rough, bad boy edge.

They were wildly in love. Diane became pregnant, they got married and Diane's parents gave them the house to officially begin their life as a married couple. Michael had come around once in a while to visit Mom before he got married. Once the grandchild arrived, they came over more often. Michael got a job in the industrial park with the help of Uncle Victor. They had a second child. When the kids started school, Michael sat with them at the kitchen table, helping them with school projects. As far as I know, Michael wasn't drinking at all once he had kids.

When their youngest started pre-school, Diane got a part time job at a pizza place around the corner from their house where she met an older guy who dressed in suits and ties and drove a Porsche. They had an affair. Things had been OK at home, but I think that Diane just wanted more out of life. Michael's roots were blue collar, working class. Diane grew up in a city that had hosted the U.S. Open. Her family was financially well off. Michael had definitely married up the socio-economic ladder. I think that Diane started comparing this new guy, who was clearly prosperous, to Michael, who came home from work with grease under his fingernails. Burlap versus silk. The bad boy image that had initially dazzled Diane had lost its luster and life had become dull for her. She told Michael that she had found someone else and wanted a divorce.

It went downhill quickly for Michael after the divorce. He was still only in his mid-twenties and ill equipped emotionally or financially to deal with the blow. He started drinking again. He lost his job. He didn't pay child support. He lived in a rented room with wiring so faulty that once when he plugged in a lamp, he was shocked so badly that he passed out.

Our father, Roger, had moved back to the Midwest, where he inherited some land a few years before. He was living with his second family in Indiana, about a two-hour drive from us. I refused to have anything to do with him, but he reconnected with the others in the family. Roger offered Michael a job working for him as a painter. My father had a large parcel of land and they built a small studio next to the main house for Michael. Supposedly, Roger had stopped drinking, but Michael was drinking hard.

About this same time, I moved to California and only saw the family a couple of times a year. Our mom and sister stayed in closer contact with Michael, though. He would come back to Mom's house for occasional visits. Over the two next decades he sank deeper and deeper into alcoholism and a life of near squalor.

Rose Ann had always been a person to do whatever she could for others. Michael knew that he would be welcome at her house any time he needed a meal or wanted money. One time, though, she turned him down and called to forewarn me that he would probably call me next. When he did call, he asked for a pretty sizable amount of money to settle a fine. He said that he was delinquent on a restitution payment and would be thrown in jail if he didn't pay. I told him no. I didn't hear from him again for many years, although he stayed in touch Rose Ann and continued to lean heavily on her generosity.

While Michael's son made it through college on scholarships and moved on to a successful career in engineering, his daughter, Colleen, was in and out of trouble with the law and had been since her teens. Kiting checks, shoplifting, drugs. She has three children, each had a different father. Since high school, she and her children had lived with Michael off and on between relationships.

Celeste Weingardt & Irene Henry

Out of Adversity, Redemption

Four years ago, Colleen was sentenced to a stint in jail and needed someone to take the children in. Her mom, Diane (Michael's ex-wife), lived nearby and was financially secure, but she had recently divorced again and was living in an adults only community. She was not interested in taking on the responsibility, which left Michael as the only available option.

When Michael took the children in, he must have had an awakening of sorts, recognizing the difference between providing a roof over their heads and being the primary caretaker. He stopped drinking cold turkey.

It has been a challenging four years for him. He had been living on his father's property rent-free and was eligible for food stamps since taking in the children, but finances were still tough as his income had always been sporadic and he had never been very motivated to work. Although Michael had been told that he would inherit the studio apartment and land he had lived in all those years, when Roger died he did not leave a written will. Roger's widow, Bonnie, was willing to sell the plot to Michael, but the asking price was far too high. He and the grandchildren moved into subsidized housing in town, the best he could do on his limited income.

In the middle of the domestic drama, Michael was diagnosed with cancer of the liver. The initial prognosis was that his condition was terminal. His son, from whom he had been estranged for years, came up from Texas and arranged for the number one surgeon at Mayo Clinic to give a second opinion. He got him a new surgery, which saved Michael's life. The doctors have sternly warned him of the danger that any drinking could do to his weakened and compromised liver.

While he's survived thanks to surgery and chemo, he is no longer able to work. Caring for the children takes up all of his limited energy. They were barely getting by on his meager disability check and food stamps. On a visit a year ago I discovered that all Michael had in his refrigerator was one bag of frozen peas, two bones for making soup stock, a half-full container of juice and a few slices of cheese. The pantry had some canned foods and some pasta. That was it for four people. His son, Rose Ann, other family members and I have started bringing groceries whenever we visit and also send packages to help out as much as we are able.

This past May, Rose Ann and I came by the apartment to drop off groceries. I smelled beer on Michael's breath when I hugged him. He said that a neighbor had brought a beer over because it was such a hot day, 104°, and that he was only drinking it to cool off. He said that he didn't know that Rose Ann was bringing me with her and that he'd never have opened the beer if he knew that I was coming, too. I can only hope that beer was a one off and not the start to him drinking again.

Rose Ann makes the four-hour round trip to bring him groceries often.

She has the children visit periodically to give Michael a break and so that they can spend time with the rest of the family. I think he would have been in far more dire straits without her. And in a way, I think him taking in the children, rescuing them like he did, saved him as much as he saved them. That meanness that was such a large part of him is gone. He's great with the children. They know he's their grandpa, but they call him Papa.

Love and support from others only goes so far, though. And those kids need him to keep making good choices.

Our Thoughts

Irene wishes that she knew more about her father's backstory to understand what forces or events shaped him into the abusive drunk that he became, but the reasons, whatever they might be, don't really matter. The damage he inflicted upon his wife and the children wouldn't have been any more or less forgivable.

When his drinking, gambling and abuse reached the point where Mary, his wife, feared for the safety of herself and her young children, she made the hard choice to divorce him in spite of the prevailing attitude of their church encouraging couples to stay together, no matter what. Being a single parent created new challenges. The children didn't receive as much supervision as she would have liked, which compounded their own challenges in growing up. Patrick was overwhelmed with the expectation that he shoulder extra responsibilities and sought refuge in joining the seminary. While Irene found a lesson of self-reliance in her mother, Rose Ann mirrored the submissive role that Mary had modeled in the early years of the father's drinking and abuse.

The damage to Michael was most lasting and pronounced. Perhaps out of guilt for feeling that she hadn't protected him from Roger's violence and Michael taking that blow intended for her, Mary was forgiving to a fault. Michael fell in with boys who were bad influences and Mary allowed Michael to get away with disrespectful behavior and juvenile infractions until ultimately, she was unable to exert any control or authority over him. Michael's acting out, drinking and mistreatment of the rest of the family members traumatized them anew.

Roger, in offering Michael a job and a place to live, initially helped his son stabilize after Diane divorced him, but it also perpetuated Michael's pattern of taking the easy way out. Roger didn't appear to be drinking any longer, but didn't appear to be doing anything to encourage Michael to stop drinking or take any other steps to pull his life together.

Both taking in the grandchildren and battling cancer paved the way for mending Michael's relationship with his son and with Irene, the last of the family to accept him back in their life. The healing process can be slow and painful, but it can happen.

BOOTS
Pat's Story

As a boy, Pat was able to count on his mother to provide basic care for himself and his siblings despite her affection for beer and an increasing distancing of herself from close relationships. As an adult, Pat resented the enabling that other family members provided and was conflicted with his own role reversal and the need to confront his mother about her drinking.

Everyone called my mother "Boots" because of the English riding boots she always wore. When she was in her early teens, she moved from Oklahoma to a small farming town in Idaho where she often rode horses over the sprawling pastures and rolling hills along the banks of the Kutnee River. She was a bright, high-spirited girl.

Her father, Roper, was half Cherokee and sold bootleg whiskey on the Cherokee Nation Reservation during prohibition. He had a good run, evading the law and making a decent profit for nine years, before his luck ran out. He was caught by the feds and sent to prison, leaving his wife, Rebecca, with six children, including Boots, and no means of support. Rebecca quickly remarried and had three more children with her new husband, a lonely widower named Pence. Combined with the six children that she had with Roper and the two that Pence had from a previous marriage, they had a grand total of 11 children. Their large, blended family moved to Idaho, where Pence had roots, shortly after they married.

Boots left school at age 16 and went to work for the family that owned the local mortuary, moving into the apartment above the funeral parlor with them. She paid her own way and was quite independent for a young, single girl of that era. My mom had a lot of pride in herself in those days. She was spunky and self-assured.

She and Charlie, my dad, married when she was 20. Her siblings and new cousins from Charlie's side of the family admired her because of her spirit and spunkiness. She stood up to Charlie's dad because of the way he treated his wife. He was kind of a jerk. He called his wife "woman" or "squaw." He'd poke her with his cane.

Charlie worked while Boots stayed home, raising babies. Little by little, life started chipping away at her confidence and sense of self-worth. They had a Pontiac that was only five years old, a pretty nice car. Mom ran it up over a curb and crashed it into a tree. No one was hurt and it didn't ruin the car, but she never drove again after that. She was only 23 at the time. For the rest of her life she was dependent on others for transportation.

My dad worked in the WPA when my parents first got married. Then he worked for the railroad and in mining. He developed diabetes when I was in the first grade and was transferred to a desk job, but he liked physical labor and hated sitting at a desk all day. He ended up quitting. He tried another mining company, but it was non-union and unsafe.

We moved from Idaho to Spokane, Washington. Charlie got a route hauling for the Spokane Gas Company. He couldn't afford a dump truck so he had to load and unload the coke – which is what is left over after burning the gas out of coal – into his pickup truck every day. It was hard physical labor that he should not have been doing. He'd get sick, insulin shock because of low blood sugar, and then as soon as he was able, he'd be back hauling. We ended up living on County services. The County program administrators got tired of Charlie being sick all the time, in and out of the hospital and unable to support our family. They put him in a business school for 18 months and he became a bookkeeper, which was less taxing on his health. He didn't like it because he thought it was sissy work, but he got used to it. He resisted going to work for any companies big enough to hire him outright – he was scornful of corporate bureaucracies — and instead picked up small odd jobs doing the books for the local service station and places like that. He also worked as a box boy at Albertson's market in the evenings to make ends meet.

Boots was a good mom. The house was always decent in spite of our poverty. I had two brothers and a sister. I was the oldest. Boots made our lunches each day, got us off to school, and had dinner on the table every night. She didn't work outside of the home; her job was taking care of the family. We were taught to be respectful and have good manners. By the time we were ten, we were responsible for making our own beds and picking up after ourselves. Mom didn't make many friends to speak of in Spokane and went to few school or community events. Her social life was with the family, which was fine by us.

Celeste Weingardt & Irene Henry

My parents weren't big drinkers in their early years together. Boots and Charlie rarely went to bars, even after my mom started drinking more. Once in a while they would go to a bar on a Saturday evening to dance, though. They both loved dancing. Sometimes they played country music on our second-hand record player and danced at home.

When I was in fourth grade, my parents started spending a lot of time with my aunt and uncle, my mom's older sister and brother-in-law. Aunt Nancy and Uncle Buck would only drink on the weekends. Uncle Buck would get several cases of beer and my parents would go over on Friday night to drink with them and then sometimes come back on Saturday night and drink some more. I remember those times as being good: lots of laughter, country music playing, dancing, and all of us having fun. My cousin was there to get into mischief with and what did we know? I wonder now how my parents were able to drive home some nights.

Buck would drink Friday night right on through to Sunday. Sunday night he would set a bottle of beer next to his bed and wake up Monday morning, drink the flat beer to straighten himself out, and then go to work and not drink again until the next weekend.

That was the beginning of unhealthy drinking for my mother. She was about 30 years old by this time. She still took good care of us and wasn't ever visibly drunk except on those weekends with Buck and Nancy. Mom was a happy drunk back then. My dad remained a cautious drinker; he had to be careful because of the diabetes.

We moved to California when I was about 14. My grandmother Rebecca had cancer and needed family to look after her. One of Mom's younger sisters also lived in the area, but she and her husband were always busy and it fell to Boots to care for their mother. My mother took a job waiting tables at a restaurant for the first couple of months after we moved because my father couldn't find work right away. That was the only time during their marriage that Mom had a job outside of the home. As soon as Charlie was able to get job, though, he made her quit. He was an 'I don't want my wife working' kind of guy.

Boots had few acquaintances and spent most days alone at home after Grandma passed. She had to wait for Dad to take her to the grocery store because it was too far to walk. By this time, she had a serious problem with low self-esteem. She had only finished her sophomore year in high school and felt that she wasn't as smart as other people. She was street smart; she just wasn't educated. She'd gotten worn down by the years when we were so poor. She had become defined by her role as wife and mother and lost confidence in herself as a separate person. I think if she had had any kind of outside influence, outside interest, it might have been a better life for her.

I didn't see any real difference between how our family was and how my friends families were. We all bought our clothes at Sears & Roebuck, Dad worked and Mom took care of the family and the house, and we listened to The Green Hornet on the radio together, just like all the other families we knew. I'm pretty sure Mom didn't drink during the day while we were at school. She did have her beer at night, but she was always up in the morning to give us breakfast and get us off to school.

My brothers, sister and I all drank by the time we were in our mid-teens. We thought it was the adult thing to do. Our parents didn't know. When I was a senior in high school, I was a cleanup boy in a meat shop, and one of the older guys there would buy booze for me. Once I had a pint of whiskey in my car and the grounds proctor – that's what they called the campus cop in those days – found it. I was sent to the principal's office and they called my mother. They told her that they found me with alcohol on campus and were threatening to expel me. She said, "Where did he get beer?" and the principle said, "Ma'am, he had a bottle of whiskey."

She was so upset! Beer was ok, but whiskey was not. She used to say that she couldn't be an alcoholic because she only drank beer. Maybe that thinking was tied to her memories of her dad selling bootleg whiskey to the Indians back during Prohibition.

I was drinking one night, showing off on my motorcycle and tried to stand up on the seat, fell and broke my arm. Not long after that I got married to wife number one. I was barely twenty years old and she was barely 18. Right away she wanted us to grow up and act like adults. She said, "We're going to be responsible. We're going to have children and you are going to get rid of that motorcycle."

I sold my motorcycle to my brother who was a couple of years younger than me. Shortly after I sold it to him, he went out drinking one night, crashed the bike and was killed. After my brother died, it changed my mother's life entirely. That's when she started serious drinking. Although she drank at home, mostly alone, she was never secretive about her drinking. My dad complained as her drinking became heavier. I would say to him, "How can you complain? If she doesn't drive a car and she doesn't have any money and you bring her the beer, how can you complain? Don't bring it." And he responded, "I couldn't live with her then." Boots was in her early forties by this point. She was still as feisty as she had been as a teen, but had developed a mean edge.

I did convince Mom to join Alcoholics Anonymous at one point when she was around 50. She lasted thirty days; she said it was just a bunch of damned old people telling their problems. The only time she didn't drink for any significant period of time was when she was in the hospital, on several extended occasions to treat her emphysema, but she would go right back to drinking as soon as she went home.

Many times Boots would wake up in the morning and say, "I'm not going to drink today." Around 10 a.m. she'd say, "I just need one beer to settle my stomach." By two o'clock I could hardly stand to be around her. She was an angry drunk, bitter and disagreeable. Yet she was still functional enough to remind my dad to have a candy bar when his sugar levels dropped too low. In spite of all the ups and downs, the years of financial struggle, there were still odd moments of tenderness between them.

My dad left her when she was 60, but even after they separated he would bring beer to her and my younger brother would drop by nearly every day to see if she had her beer, you know, to keep her happy. It was easier for them than getting angry phone calls and having to deal with her sour moods.

A year after my parents separated, Mom commit suicide. She took pills washed down with a fifth of vodka. To my knowledge, she never drank vodka and she never abused pills any other time. Just the once. She had saved them up.

Looking back, I wish that I had been more forceful about Alcoholics Anonymous or counseling, or some kind of professional help. I don't know how bright, high-spirited, spunky Boots got so lost. It seemed to me that, for many years, her only ambition in life was to sit with her legs tucked under her on the couch, smoking cigarettes and drinking a beer and wearing a hole in the couch. Feeling that everybody was better than she was, better off than she was, and living better lives than she was. She had a sad life.

My brother, Bud, became an alcoholic, too, just like our mother was. Bud is 69 now and has stopped drinking only because of his poor health and being scared by the doctor's warning of what will happen if he keeps drinking. It's been a rough life, but I can't save him. I believe that each of us needs to live our own life. I'm the kind of person who says, "That's how it is. I can't change it. I've got to keep moving." It's my wildebeest theory: If you stay around long enough, something will get you, so you just have to keep a good attitude and keep moving. If I slow down for my brother, I could be brought down, too.

Our Thoughts

Pat remarked several times that, although she drank heavily, his mother always managed to keep an orderly house and attend to the family's basic needs. A typical description of a functioning alcoholic — one who maintains just enough control over their drinking to keep up the appearance of managing responsibilities. What Pat does not address so directly was the role model that he and his siblings had in her. They all drank in their teens. Pat broke his arm attempting a foolish and dangerous stunt on a motorcycle while drunk. His brother was killed driving while intoxicated. The youngest brother has been an alcoholic and drug abuser his whole life.

Pat wishes that he had done more to help his mom to get sober. At the same time, he also acknowledges the limited influence we have on others. We hope that Pat takes some comfort in knowing that he, unlike other family members, did make some attempt to connect her with resources to combat the alcoholism. He can sympathize with her thwarted opportunities in life and the fact that most of the family abetted her drinking by being her suppliers, but it was never his responsibility to save her from herself.

THE PATRIARCH
Irma J's Story

Fueled by internal pressure to prove his worth and to overcome the feelings of abandonment by his own parents, this father worked hard all of his life to be a good man, a good father, a good employer, one who took care of others.

My father Arturo's parents divorced when he was two years old. This was shocking in the Mexican American community in the 1930s. His father took off for parts unknown and his mother, too young to care for a child on her own, left him with his grandparents and moved to San Fernando. She remarried and had another son and a daughter but did not have Arturo join her new family. His mother was very strict with him, abusive, when she did see him.

Arturo grew up on his grandparents ranch in Somis in a loving environment, feeling more like a younger brother of his aunts and uncles than a nephew. He was very close to his grandmother and adored her. He was an intelligent child and a born leader. He was treated as an equal by his aunts and uncles by the time he reached his teens, even though he was a number of years their junior.

My parents married when Arturo was 24 and my mother, Ana, was 20. Arturo became a nurseryman. An uncle taught him how to graft lemon trees and provided him with a small section of ranch land to grow seedlings and start his business. He was a smart businessman as well as a talented arborist, successful enough to hire a crew to do the physical labor while he focused on expanding his fledgling business.

IN THE DRINK

Even though my father was younger than the other adults in our family, he became the patriarch, the head of the clan. He was intelligent and wasn't preachy. The family came to him for advice. They respected him. His uncle's considered him their equal.

We moved into town a few years after I was born. I have a brother who is a year and a half older than I am, and three younger siblings who were each born five years apart. So there are 19 years between the oldest and the youngest. I always felt provided for. When I was young, my father had a carpenter friend build a playhouse for me complete with running water and electricity.

We adored Dad; Mom less so. She was the family disciplinarian. (Dad didn't have to. He could scare us just with a look.) In those times, in our culture, things were very patriarchal. Fathers ruled.

Mom always served Dad and took care of the household. Dad used to joke with us daughters, especially when he had been drinking, "Don't you ever let any son of a bitch mistreat you, make you subservient." When we asked about how he treated Mother, he said, "That's different." He always thought of her as a country girl because she came from Piru, a tiny rural community. My dad finished 11th grade, a high achievement in the Mexican culture for his generation. Mom only went through 6th grade because where she grew up only had an elementary school and her father wouldn't allow his daughters to go to the next town over to attend high school. Dad did not feel that Mom was on a par with him intellectually, but he did often discuss news and politics with me. He was encouraging and supportive of us kids. He urged us to do well in school, to be informed about local and world events, to form our own opinions.

My parents would have shouting matches. She would always start them: he was always out, he was spending too much money, his drinking, how the marriage was all one sided.

Dad was mostly a weekend drinker when I was young. He and his drinking buddies liked to go to the Hitching Post in Old Camarillo. Dad would get boisterous, joking, more extraverted when he drank. I did see him falling down drunk on occasion, but most of the time he would drive himself home. They all drove drunk in those days. If they got pulled over, the police would usually just instruct them to drive straight home.

On the weekends our family used to drive the treacherous, winding back road over Grimes Canyon to Fillmore to visit family. My mom, who never had a driver's license, would steer while my drunken dad controlled the gas. It was a terrifying ride for us kids. Many times Mom would call Maria and Hector, her friends in Fillmore, for a ride. One of them would drive our car and the other would follow in their own for the return trip. I might owe my life to them.

We lived in a tight neighborhood. Everybody knew everybody. Both of our parents had many friends. Through school, I made many friends from different backgrounds, but our community, the neighborhood in which I lived, was all Mexican-American. There were constant parties and celebrations. Mom would drink a beer at social events or on a hot evening. Dad drank whiskey. He had a little flask, his "Baby Doll". Sometimes he would be shaky in the morning before he'd had a drink of whiskey.

When Dad was in his fifties, he developed diabetes. He changed his eating habits. He tried to stop drinking many times. He would stop for a year, sometimes two, but he'd always start drinking again.

My parents moved to the Central Valley when my father retired. Four or five years after they moved I was having a difficult pregnancy. It was two weeks before my due date and I was on complete bed rest when my mother called to let me know that Dad was in the hospital. Cirrhosis. They didn't think he was going to make it through the night. I lay flat in the back seat of the car the whole way out and back so that I could see him one more time. Happily, he survived that night and so did my baby.

After the hospital episode he was sober for four years before he started drinking again. A few years later he was diagnosed with cancer. I was alarmed with the drinking, knowing about the danger with both the cirrhosis and the diabetes, but the doctor told me that he didn't have much time left, so why deprive him of a beer or two? I agreed.

Our Thoughts

The narrator went out of her way to say that she never blamed her father for his drinking, that he was always a good father. And yet, when she was relating the story of being in the car on the dangerous mountain road with her drunken father behind the wheel, she clearly remembered the sense of terror she had known those many years ago. She understood at that young age, just as she knows now as a grown woman, that her father had repeatedly put the entire family's lives in jeopardy. But how do you allow yourself to be angry with someone that you love? How do you partition off the bad behavior – the drunk driving – from the man who was mostly kind and loving to you?

She also deflected blame onto cultural norms of the day. Heavy drinking and the dismissive way in which he treated his wife were perfectly acceptable, even expected, as long as they were hardworking, honest men who provided for their families.

Fathers often stand tall upon a pedestal in their children's eyes. When their idol topples —as they normally do at some point during the teen years - the child can begin to see their parent as a mere mortal. When they stay atop the pedestal beyond that, there has to be a little bit of wishful thinking and denial of reality. But, as she said about not depriving her dad of a beer or two when he was so close to the end of his life, what does it really matter? She loved him, and for her that was enough.

Celeste Weingardt & Irene Henry

THE ILLUSION OF A PRIVILEGED LIFE
Gail's Story

Burdened with a crushing sense of self-inflicted guilt and misplaced responsibility for her mother's drinking, this daughter continues to be weighted down by the relationship long after her alcoholic mother left this earth.

Everyone called my parents Betty and Doc, including me. They took pleasure in being thought of as unconventional, avant-garde, a touch eccentric. Doc, especially, thrived on the intellectual stimulation of philosophical discussions. My parents had an enviable social life, even though my father, who was condescending and elitist could be difficult to be around. There were frequent parties and their crowd drank liberally. The men favored Manhattans and Tom Collins. The women preferred Champagne Cocktails and Daiquiris. Betty had a closet overflowing with the latest chic fashions, which she wore to good effect with her slim figure and inherent sophistication.

Betty had met Doc at the Rochester Institute of Technology while studying to be a dietitian. Doc, who was four years older, was teaching in the sciences department at the time. There were imbalances in their relationship from the start. Betty grew up in a small farming town outside of Rochester, New York, the oldest of four daughters. The family wasn't truly poor, but definitely of modest means. Doc came from a banking family of substantial financial resources. He had already earned a degree at MIT before he and my mother met. He went on to obtain his PhD after they married, but Betty never completed her fourth year of studies to secure her bachelor's degree, instead sublimating her education and career plans to be supportive of Doc's own ambitions.

Doc was a domineering personality, dictating where he and Betty would go and whom they would spend time with, always imposing his will. My mother was pliable; she was an agreeable, socially generous, lovely woman. In many ways, Doc depended on Betty to be his counter-balance. While he undeniably possessed a certain personal magnetism, it was easier for others to spend time with him when my mother was at his side. My father didn't get along with many people, in his personal or professional life, and didn't try to. He taught at several universities over the years, and flaunted his authority. He would say things like, "I had to flunk that kid because his breath smelled like peanut butter." I'm sure it wasn't true, but he liked to tell those kinds of stories. He didn't like to talk to you unless you were smart, and he didn't think many people were. He didn't think Betty was particularly intelligent.

I grew up knowing that my parents had not intended to have children. My father blamed Betty for being careless in getting pregnant. My mother had rheumatic fever when she was young and was told that her heart wasn't strong enough to have children, so when Doc married her he thought that she had made a promise to him that there wouldn't be any babies. But whether Betty planned the pregnancy or not, I came along. My father was further disappointed that he had a daughter instead of a son who he could at least have molded in his image.

Neither of my parents was warm or affectionate with me. They didn't say, "I love you". When I started my period, my father stopped calling me "the brat" and began calling me "the young lady". When my first husband asked for my hand in marriage, my father just harrumphed and pulled up the newspaper he was reading. Didn't even acknowledge the question.

I adored my father, though. I cherished what attention he did give me. I believe that he loved me dearly, although he didn't show it directly. He enjoyed teaching me random facts like how gasoline made a car run or showing me a clever trick to solve a mathematic equation. In my teens, Doc taught me how to fly an airplane and we built a car together.

Most people were intimidated by him. My mother and I were, too, in our own ways. Yet we were also in a weird sort of unspoken competition for his attention and affection as far back as I remember. Sadly, that rivalry caused a lot of tension between us, especially during my teens.

In my first true memories, around the time I started kindergarten, I remember my mother being happy. We lived at the time in Washington, DC, in a beautifully appointed downtown apartment. Betty and her circle of friends were enthusiastically involved with the Red Cross and other aid organizations. Life was a whirlwind of parties and charity balls. They socialized mostly with Doc's peers and their wives: academics, intellectuals and the social elite. Although Betty came from a modest background, she had natural poise and sense of style and was easily able to fit in.

We moved to rural Maryland a few years later, and a few years after that, moved again to Oxnard, California. My father had been offered the position of chief scientist for the Pacific Missile Range at Point Mugu naval base. He was brilliant in his work, but as I was told many years later by one of his former co-workers when I was delivering his personal papers for the official archives, my father was "a real son-of-a-bitch who only worked on what he wanted to do, not necessarily what he was supposed to do."

My parents inserted themselves into the middle of the local social scene, throwing elaborate parties. It wasn't just the parties, though. It seemed like there was alcohol on offer anytime. I remember coming home from elementary school to find one of the top ranking officers from the base reclining in my father's Naugahyde easy chair, drinking Apple Jack straight out of the bottle.

I first noticed my mother's drinking around the time I started Jr. High. She would have bridge games in the afternoon with her friends. She would be acting silly when I got home from school, wanting to dance with me, twirling me around and around, laughing when I asked her to stop. Betty worked at being very thin and was always dieting, so any alcohol would go straight to her head. She was probably drinking too much, but it was within social convention.

It wasn't until later, as Father started to travel more, amid suspicions (although there was never any real proof) that he was having an affair with his secretary, that Mother began drinking to excess. She seemed to be very lonely. We lived far away from any family, and rarely saw relatives, Mother's three sisters, or Father's brother and sister. Even though she was drinking heavily by this time, she continued to be active in the community. She was the head of the PTA. She started a group on base called The Missile Mrs. for the women associated with Point Mugu.

When I had slumber parties, Mother would often join in with my girlfriends and me. She tried hard to be 'one of the girls.' It was awkward and embarrassing for me, but my friends didn't mind because she would give us cigarettes. My friends thought she was a cool mother.

For my sixteenth birthday, Betty took my friend and me to Catalina Island, checked us into the hotel and then disappeared. We went into town on our own, but got scared by a couple of older guys who started bothering us. We went back to the hotel and locked the doors and stayed there, freaked out, all night. My mother didn't show up until the next day. She had an excuse of some sort, but I can't remember what it was. I don't recall my mother asking me not to tell my father, but I never did. I was certainly angry with my mother, but must have understood the ramifications of his knowing without having to be told.

Perhaps Betty felt that she needed her own adventure, that life was passing her by. Mother had been raised on a farm and had little social experience before getting married. She never talked about having had another boyfriend before she met my father. While I was still in high school, my mother would sometimes bring home sailors from the nearby base for me to meet. I had no interest in any of them. She loved to take me shopping and would buy me clothes. I remember a purple sweater, too tight for my taste, very revealing. She loved it on me but I was uncomfortable to be seen wearing it. Maybe she wanted to live vicariously through me.

In reaction to my mother's intrusions into my personal life, I did a lot of acting out. When Doc and Betty would go on trips, I drank. I would hotwire Doc's car and take it out for joy rides.

My relationship with my mother really started to fray by the time I got to college. Betty came up to visit me for Mother's Day weekend during my freshman year at Berkeley. She hadn't told me that she was coming and I refused to change my plans. So she traveled all that way and spent most of the weekend alone. Shortly after that failed connection, my parents moved back to the northeast and she was no longer close enough to pop in for weekend visits. I feel so badly about that now. I think she was feeling very lonely after I left for college and had thought I would be as happy to see her as she was to see me.

I got pregnant while I was still at Berkeley. The father wasn't anyone I wanted to marry and abortion was not an option for me. I finished the semester, then Betty came out to California to get me and we drove back to New York together. We gave an acquaintance of mine a ride to Chicago, precluding discussion about the pregnancy while he was in the car, and I continued to keep silent about it the rest of the way home. We both made an effort to keep the conversation light to make the drive bearable. Once we got back in Rochester, it all came out. I remember one screaming match we had while driving in downtown Rochester. She called me a bitch. She told me I was wasting my life. Her words cut deeply. Believe me, I had already learned my lesson and did not need the lectures and condemnation. We fought a lot after that. It hurt her very much that I had gotten pregnant. She acted as though it was somehow a personal rebuke directed at her. I think she felt abandoned, that she no longer could talk to me. She used to think of me as an ally and a friend and she couldn't see me that way any longer.

I was sent to live with relatives out of state for the remainder of my pregnancy and gave the baby up for adoption before returning to New York. I was gone for several months, and Betty's drinking seemed much worse when I got back. I think that my father held my mother responsible for my getting pregnant and took his anger out on her. I hold myself partly responsible for her alcoholism because of the added stress my personal crisis caused.

Plus, she missed California and her friends. Doc had been a big wheel in Oxnard, and by extension, she was, too. In Rochester, with its considerably larger population, they didn't they have the same social cache.

Meanwhile, I was getting my life back on track. I enrolled in the local college that spring and brought my grades up, enabling me to transfer to the University of Rochester. The next year I met Jim and we quickly fell in love. We originally planned to get married in June but moved the wedding date up to March because I was so distraught about living at home. The atmosphere was constantly tense. Doc would nag Betty to slow down her drinking and she would turn around and accuse me of having the drinking problem. Absolutely not true and Father knew it. There were several occasions when I had to pick Betty up from a bar because she was falling down drunk. A couple of times I found her passed out. It was intensely embarrassing to me. At the same time, it was also painful to see that alcohol had become more important to her than anything else in her life. When she was sober, she was still a lovely person. She had never been a particularly warm person, but she had always been charming and amiable. When she was drunk, she would drool. She was unsteady and would bump into furniture. She would laugh inappropriately. She was horrible to be around.

I was so worried that my mother would ruin my wedding day, I asked Doc to have an intervention. In that setting, we both told her that we felt she was drinking too much. For the first time, she didn't deny that she had a drinking problem. She told us she would stop. But she didn't. When I would talk to her, attempting to understand what was going on, she blamed the drinking on how worried she got about Doc. Doc's toys were always kind of dangerous; he had the airplane, sailboats, the motorcycle, the super fast Jaguar XKE. Plus he was always the center of attention, so I think that Betty had this sense of living in his shadow. It didn't help that my parents continued to socialize mostly with people who were also copious drinkers.

Over the course of the next several years, we attempted other interventions. Doc put Betty in the hospital a few times to help her get sober, but she had no real desire to stop drinking.

My parents moved to Los Altos, California, not long after I got married. Betty only visited me once during those years. She came to stay with me when my first daughter was born; what should have been an occasion of joy and of bonding. One morning, I was going to take my shower and walked into the kitchen to tell my mother to not to use the water for a few minutes, and there she was, holding my four-day-old baby casually in one arm and swigging a bottle of Crème de Cocoa. I said, "I'm sorry. You have to go." I made her leave.

Doc and Betty bought a beautiful sailboat and took it out often. They were both competent sailors with many years of experience, yet Betty was still fearful out on the water. The two of them were out sailing one unexceptional day with no strong winds or adverse weather conditions. The sailboat's boom swung around and hit Betty in the head. The blow caused a detached retina in her right eye. Betty waited for a day and a half before she saw a doctor because she didn't understand how serious the injury was. By the time she sought treatment, the damage was irreversible and she went blind in that eye. It took months of therapy for her to learn to adjust to the loss.

They moved again, this time to St. Petersburg, Florida, and lived on another gorgeous sailing sloop for a few years. Jim and I visited them several times with our two young daughters. They always seemed fine. Betty was managing with her reduced vision and, as always, they had cultivated a small circle of friends and had a lively social life. Continuing their nomad lifestyle, my father was offered an opportunity to work for NATO in Italy and they moved to Italy for three years. Father had English-speaking co-workers but Betty had a miniscule pool of people with whom she was able to interact due to the language barrier. Everything seemed OK as far as I could glean, though, from intermittent phone conversations and letters.

When Doc retired, they returned to Florida and settled in Yankeetown. I was surprised at the type of people they were spending time with. It was primarily neighbors who weren't the usual intellectuals and academics that my father had always preferred. But my parents seemed happy enough. Doc set up a small business, bartering his mechanical skills for fish and shrimp. They didn't need the money. He just enjoyed fixing boat engines. He also taught occasional classes at the local university.

To our horror, on a boating trip up the coast to Massachusetts, Betty was hit again on the side of the head with a sailboat boom and her other retina detached. The doctors attempted to save her vision but damage was too extensive and she gradually lost all vision. I have speculated endlessly on how this possibly could have happened to her twice. Was she drunk? Was my father not paying attention – or worse, somehow responsible? Did Betty's anxiety about boating grow to be such an irrational fear that she subconsciously caused the accident? The most likely scenario was that they had both been drinking and she just didn't get out of the way in time. She went to rehab for three months and learned to live as a blind person, but it was hard. She didn't complain much, but when she did, it was heart wrenching. Doc did allow her to continue drinking some, doling it out according to his whims.

When my father died of prostate cancer, within a few months of his diagnosis, Mother was adamant that she stay in Florida and remain independent. At this point, I had divorced my husband and moved to Albany, New York. I hired a succession of housekeepers to take care of her but none seemed to work out. The first one couldn't stand her drinking and the second got her drunk, put her to bed and would then take off, leaving her without a helper. The third one stole from her, sometimes writing checks that Betty thought were for $50 but was for much more.

When the fourth caretaker finally said she could no longer manage my mother, Betty came, very reluctantly, to stay with me in Albany. It was hard for both of us. I had a full-time job and Mother was at a loss because she couldn't see. Our three-story brick rowhouse was hard for her to navigate. She still smoked and became so stressed at times that she would smoke alone. There were a burn marks on the rugs and I was afraid she would burn the place down. She was also drinking again, having the liquor and cigarettes delivered. I had no idea where she was finding the money to buy them. She wanted me to quit my job and stay home with her, but I couldn't afford to.

During these months, we also were able to experience some good times, she and I both having matured and mellowed. My daughter reminded me the other day that I said at one point, "Now she's just a sweet old lady!"

When I was no longer able to provide proper care for Betty, she went into a nursing home. It was horrible. The staff would tie her to a chair so she wouldn't wander and she was given drugs to keep her calm. Betty no longer had access to alcohol, but the drugs, in the excessive amounts she was given, were worse. When Betty was hospitalized with pneumonia and given a thorough health examination, the nursing home staff was alerted to the problem the drugs were causing and promptly weaned her off. At the same time, I found a social worker to help me find the right kind of place for her. She was moved into an assisted living facility, where she was much happier. She found a boyfriend, a dapper elderly gentleman, was allowed to smoke, and was quite content until she passed after succumbing to a stroke.

I've thought so much about my mother in the years following her death. I feel I never knew her well. That was partly my fault; my father was a dominating, controlling person and I wanted to please him, and by doing so, often ignored my mother. It was primarily because of her drinking, though. I didn't understand why she allowed herself to be sloppy and stupid and it revolted me. Other people all around us drank and managed to keep up a decent presence. As I said, I was pretty self-centered during the years I lived with my parents.

How have I managed? I've had periods where I abused drinking myself. My first husband is a recovering alcoholic. One of my daughters asked me to send her to rehab when she was 19. She got blackout drunk and was scared to death that she would be an alcoholic like her father and grandmother. I'm relieved and grateful that she never drank again after rehab. I also don't drink anymore and feel so much better both physically and mentally. I've had a lot of therapy. Each of the therapists has told me that my mother's alcoholism wasn't in any way my fault, but I can't help but think that I could have done things differently. I wish I had tried harder to understand. The only time I could talk to her about her drinking, though, was when she was sober, and when she was sober I don't think I would have trusted her to tell me the truth.

I tend to forget the bad and remember the good. That has been a mixed blessing because I would like to remember my mother better than I do. At the same time, blocking, forgetting, helped me cope with times that were hard. Which is better? The sad thing is, perhaps if I remembered more, I wouldn't be able to forgive myself for not being a better daughter.

Our Thoughts

Young Betty's plans for a college degree and career, abandoned for what she no doubt thought would be an exciting life among the educated and well-to-do, turned out to be a life in a supporting role with few speaking lines. Lonely, disillusioned and unfulfilled, Betty turned to drinking and occasional departures from propriety: flirting, giving cigarettes to her daughter and her daughter's friends, disappearing overnight and leaving two scared teenage girls to fend for themselves.

Betty no doubt believed for a long time that her drinking was no different than anyone else's. Not having alcohol as the centerpiece of all social activities may or may not have helped Betty control her drinking, but certainly having it ever present contributed to her dependence on alcohol to soften the edges of her disappointments.

Gail has placed blame for much of her mother's downfall on herself for not having treated her well. She spoke of having competed with her mother for her father's affections. That this dynamic existed was the fault of both parents – the Adults, not the child's. Gail feels guilty for having been mean to her mom during her teens. We ask, what teenager is not? From all that Gail shared, the manner in which she treated her mother never exceeded the normal boundaries of an adolescent's rebellion.

Yes, Betty ended up blind, helpless and alone, and while we believe that Doc should have been kinder and more supportive of his wife, it was never Gail's responsibility to have provided Betty with a better life. In sharing her story with us, and with her children, Gail is hoping to find some clarity and peace about the complicated relationship that she had with her mother, a woman she loved. Her mother is no longer alive and able to forgive Gail; if forgiveness is even called for, Gail is left to find forgiveness within hersel

Parents of alcoholics

Guilt, second-guessing and a huge sense of failed responsibility dominate the special hell many parents of alcoholics inhabit. Sometimes, buried under these self-castigations, there is embarrassment, too; a fear that others will judge them and think less of them for their child's behavior.

Take an honest and unflinching look at how you influenced your child's life choices. If there are things that you need to apologize for, do so. If there are wrongs you can right, do that, too. If you've taken a hard look and feel that factors outside of your control were the root cause, you can still be part of the solution. It starts with an open conversation originating from a place of love, one that sets aside the urge to blame or lecture. You can promise to be there for them on the road to recovery, but be wary of enabling. Acknowledge the past, but don't dwell on it.

At some point children become adults who must make their own life choices, take responsibility and deal with the consequences of their actions. You probably will never stop loving or caring about your child, but you will have to let go. And then it's up to them.

Celeste Weingardt & Irene Henry

IDENTITY CROSSROADS
Sandy's Story

Her son's drinking, disrespectfulness and serial bad choices created the hardest personal challenge this mom has ever faced.

Kyle's problem, much like his dad's, is that he doesn't know when to stop drinking once he starts. Kyle tries to make excuses for his drinking. He tells his dad, "You drink, so I drink, too." I think, in a way, Kyle is both trying to blame his dad for his drinking, but also might be looking for understanding.

There had been a period when my husband, Tom, had been drinking heavily. He got a DUI when Kyle was a sophomore in high school. Tom sobered up, but Kyle started drinking around this time.

I remember one time about a year after he graduated from high school, after we'd kicked him out of the house twice already, had let him come back each time after we cooled off. Kyle wanted the keys to the car and I was the only one home with him. I knew he had been drinking. We were in the stairwell and he came up behind me and grabbed my arm and yanked it behind me, braced me up against the wall and said, "You need to give me the fucking keys." When I told him no, he said, "I'll just hold you up against this wall and keep twisting your arm until you give them up." He'd been like that since high school, since he starting drinking and doing drugs. He didn't have control over his temper when he'd been drinking.

His sister, Megan, was leaving for Brazil to do a school year abroad. Kyle came to the house for the going away party and was completely drunk. He had a water bottle full of gin. He flipped out so bad that his friend

Reese basically sat on him until he calmed down. Kyle moved up to Sonoma to live with Reese for a while after that. Reese was attending Sonoma State. We were hoping that if Kyle had a change of environment, a change of friends, it would put him on a better path. We covered his expenses with the idea that hanging out with friends who were going to college would motivate him to enroll, too.

He and Reese went to a party where they had some beers or what have you. They decided to walk home because they had been drinking. It was miles away and one in the morning. They only had three dollars between them. Not enough to afford a cab. Kyle started ringing doorbells. The police were called and the boys got tossed in jail for disturbing the peace.

So Kyle's time in Sonoma, the change of environment, didn't help as we had hoped. But I don't think it made things any worse than they would have been if he had stayed here.

A few months later, on Super Bowl Sunday, Kyle went up to a party in San Luis Obispo with a bunch of friends. Around midnight we got a call that Kyle was in the hospital. His friends told us that they weren't sure what he had drunk or what pills he had taken, but he had passed out and they couldn't wake him up. He had urinated on himself. Two of his friends held him under his arms and tried to walk him around the parking lot, but still couldn't get him to wake up. One kid said they should just let him sleep it off, but luckily they ended up taking him to the hospital. He was just percentage points away from complete alcohol poisoning when they brought him in.

It took us two hours to drive to San Luis Obispo, followed by several more tense hours in the emergency room before he was stabilized and we were able to drive him home. There's this 151-proof drink called Everclear, which is so potent that it is illegal to sell in several states. Apparently, Kyle had been drinking that and beer plus took some pills.

Another time, after our daughter was back living at home and going to college following her year in Brazil, Kyle was so drunk and acting horribly that Tom told him he couldn't stay at our house that night. (Yes, we had let him move back in once again.) After the rest of us retired for the evening, Kyle came back, picked out a large bamboo stick from the yard and started hitting our bedroom window and yelling at two in the morning. Yelling at the top of his lungs, "Let me in!" We didn't let him in and eventually he stopped banging on the window. We discovered the next morning that he ended up sleeping on a deck chair in the backyard.

Kyle got a DUI shortly after he turned twenty-one. Tom and I talked at length about how to handle Kyle and how to be on the same page. We struggled with questions about how to make a healthier family situation; what would be helpful, and, when did our efforts cross over into enabling? We went, as a family, to counseling with a therapist who specialized in younger people with alcohol and drug addictions. The counselor gave us really good ideas to implement like posting our house rules on the refrigerator, which we did. A lot of it was addressing Kyle's general behavior. Basic things like showing some consideration to my husband and me; not cussing, picking up after himself. Little things. He told Kyle that when he felt like he was going to lose his temper, he should leave the house. Go walk until he calmed down.

Six months later, Kyle was charged with a second DUI. The second was far more significant. It happened between six and seven a.m. Kyle lost control of the car and crashed into a lamppost, which luckily took the brunt of the impact, protecting two children on the sidewalk from severe bodily injury. The district attorney charged Kyle with a felony DUI because one of the children did receive some minor injuries.

After the second DUI, Kyle had to go to court. The DA in Santa Barbara County doesn't budge on DUI's; does not negotiate the charges. We hired an attorney who told us that if Kyle voluntarily entered a formal rehab program it could count as time served, so Kyle decided that if it would save him from going to jail, he would go to Vista Del Mar, which at the time was a nine a.m. to three p.m. commitment for seven consecutive days. He also was required to go to AA meeting and other group meetings.

That program did not satisfy the court terms, however. On the recommendation of his lawyer, Kyle entered the Salvation Army rehab in Pasadena, one of the officially recognized programs in the area. It seemed to me that he went solely to avoid jail, not because he believed he had a drinking problem, so he was just marking time. The Salvation Army is a six-month program with a strong Christian component and is very regimented with precise times for waking and meals, prayer time every morning, work assignments all day and church every Sunday. Sometimes Kyle would comment that it was too religious for him. Also extremely controlling. He had to put in a special request just to go off property for lunch with us on the day he received his ninety-day sobriety chip.

He got kicked out a month before he completed rehab – accused of stealing some jewelry from the donation bin — so none of the time in rehab counted toward time served. There was insufficient evidence for formal charges, but they kicked him out anyway.

The District Attorney's office was willing to look at work furlough if Kyle was in school full time and working. His attorney highly suggested that as the route to go. The only other option was jail. Kyle re-enrolled at Santa Barbara College and already had a job at Gino's Pizza. It took a while, but when it was all said and done, he was sentenced to work furlough for six months. He had to stay sober throughout that stint, plus through the probation term after he was released. They did random drug and urine tests. Once he came home, they would also do unannounced visits to our home

IN THE DRINK

where they would look through his room, just toss it. Three officers would come. One stayed outside while the other two went through his stuff.

Kyle worked and went to school. He took mass transit. We got him a motorized bicycle that did not require a driver's license to operate. He improved in his respectfulness to the family from a one - being the lowest on the scale - to a three or four. He still had a mouth on him. But it was only verbal at this point, not physically abusive.

He drank a couple of times after the second DUI, but couldn't risk it during the time he was being monitored by the system. Once he completed the terms of probation, there were new incidences of his drinking and a return to disrespectful behavior, especially to me, telling me to 'shut the eff up' and things like that. I have been told that people lash out at those closest to them because they look at you as the safe person, the one who will let them get away with it. A lot of times I tried to just ignore those outbursts, to let it go.

There came a point when we needed to take back our own quality of life, however. I didn't want to come home to this anymore. My husband and I had been willing to go to counseling, to put in the time and the money to get Kyle healthier. But that's only part of the equation. Kyle needed to make a commitment, too. Things were getting worse, not better, at home. We kicked him out of the house, resolving as a united front not to allow him back again this time.

He went to live with his girlfriend, Amber, and her family. After work furlough, she had broken up with him for several months but they got back together. And now she was pregnant. Kyle really stepped up, grew up, after Amber became pregnant. After their son, Elliot, was born, Amber had to go back to work. She wanted to go back to school to complete her associates' degree and encouraged Kyle to take night classes with her. Amber's parents watched the baby when Amber and Kyle were at work; Tom and I worked out a schedule to help take care of the baby a couple of evenings each week so they could go to school. To my knowledge, Kyle wasn't drinking. He could even talk about it with a sense of humor. Everyone was getting along. It was a good year for everyone in the family.

Six months ago, when people were in town for Elliot's christening, Kyle, Reese, a cousin and some other friends went to a local micro-brew taproom where they did samplers. When he came home and it was obvious to me that he had been drinking, I called him on it. Kyle insisted that he could do a small sampler and be fine. I said, "No. You are an alcoholic. You don't get a bye. There are no exceptions."

Amber was more upset that Kyle had lied to her. He initially denied that he had been drinking. She told him, "I can smell the beer on your breath."

A few months ago, Kyle and his little family moved in with Tom and me as Amber's parents had to do some extensive repairs on their home. This was intended to be a short-term proposition. Initially, Kyle was fairly OK although I had some issues with him acting like a guest instead of pitching in to help around the house. After I called a family meeting and we talked it out, he and Amber started at least clearing their own dishes and taking care of their laundry, vacuuming the living room once in a while; more like roommates than family, but still better.

Kyle does not do well under stress. Shortly after they moved in with us, he was looking to change jobs and trying to negotiate pay. I knew that was stressful for him, but when I heard him yelling at Amber, I went downstairs and told Kyle that yelling was not allowed in this house, that he needed to speak respectfully. I let Amber know that she was welcome to sleep upstairs in the guest room if she wanted.

Amber told Kyle, "When you're in a temper, you don't listen to me. You yell right in my face and I don't want to be talked to that way. You need to deal with your temper issues." She and the baby ended up going to her parent's house.

That first night after they left, Kyle acted like he was thinking, "Yay! I'm free." No having to get up in the middle of the night to change diapers. But by the second night it seemed like he realized how much he missed his family. He went to see Amber a couple of times, had dinner with her and talked it out. She came back three days later.

He gets defensive when he falls off the wagon. Just last weekend, he had a beer when he was out with his friend Connor. Amber was pissed with him. She told him, "No, you're not allowed to drink and drive at all." Kyle said that she and I were making too big of a deal out of it. Amber needed to leave for work at that point, cutting the exchange short. The argument between them picked up again at dinner the following evening. Amber wanted to draw me into the conversation to back her up.

I said to Kyle, "Here's the thing. We told you that you could only live in this house if you're alcohol and drug free. If you believe that you are going to have an issue with drinking, my suggestion is that you go check out AA meetings. If you're finding it difficult to maintain your sobriety, go find a resource to help you out. You don't have to do it on your own."

I think Kyle is at a crossroads. He could go either way. Stay sober, be a family man, get a college degree. He'd like to start his own landscaping business someday. He's already done a lot of the legwork to get the felony DUI reduced to a misdemeanor so that he is eligible for the required licenses. Or he could start drinking again and destroy all that potential for a really good life. It's up to him.

IN THE DRINK

Our Thoughts

Life has been a roller coaster for Sandy for many years now. Just when she thought the family has stabilized when her husband stopped drinking, Kyle started his unfortunate journey with alcohol. His occasional drug use, substance-fueled angry outbursts and constant disrespect created immense household tension.

Sandy and Tom have struggled to find the right response, to give Kyle support without enabling, to keep a united front. They bailed him out of jail and dealt with the court system on his behalf. They footed the bill for hospitals, lawyers and rehab. They gave him a roof over his head.

When Kyle's presence in the house became too disruptive to ignore or the transgressions too great to forgive, they attempted to withdraw the privilege of living in their home. Yet, as parents, it is heartbreaking to know that your child has nowhere else to go and they were quick to give him second chances with the slimmest of apologies and promises for better behavior.

This unhealthy dynamic has gone on for nearly a decade. At some point, Sandy and Tom really do need to take their home back, once and for all.

Sandy has tried to be supportive. She has tried to help Kyle recognize how his problem with alcohol is directly linked to most of his difficulties. She has attempted to steer him toward resources that could help him with both his alcohol abuse and anger issues.

Kyle has the ability to turn his life around. He also has the potential to destroy everything that he's got going for himself. We hope that Sandy can weather the emotional storm if Kyle chooses poorly.

Celeste Weingardt & Irene Henry

LOST AT 40
Robin's Story

According to this stepmother, the drinking started as an act of defiance and a reaction to neglect as a pre-teen, stunting the normal maturing process and contributing to a life of reduced opportunity. Life threatening health issues caused by the years of excessive drinking may still not be enough to keep her husband's stepson away from the bottle.

As an infant Mitchell learned to sleep through the nightly screaming matches, his parents too involved in their own crazy drama to hear his cries. His parents divorced when he was three and Mitchell never saw his father again. There were no phone calls or birthday cards. Mitchell couldn't recall his father's face by the time he entered grade school. In those turbulent years after the divorce, Mitchell felt like an afterthought to his mother, Suzanne, who was focused on her own needs. There were no other adults in his life for him to turn to for care or comfort. He grew to be a low-spirited child and never really fit in well with others.

There was one small light in Mitchell's life. He was artistically talented and spent many hours drawing. On long, lonely evenings in his early adolescent years, he would fill page upon page in his sketch pad, cranking up the volume on the radio for company and turning on lights throughout the house, temporarily holding at bay anxiety and loneliness while his mother was out.

When he was 12 years old, Suzanne remarried and soon had another son. Mitchell was assigned to babysit his infant half-brother whenever his mother and new stepfather, John, went out. Full or resentment and anger,

IN THE DRINK

Mitchell decided that if they were going to take away his childhood, then dammit, he was plenty old enough to drink – and alcohol was always readily available in the home.

Mitchell's mom and step dad, John (who is now my husband), divorced after a brief marriage. John couldn't take the constant battles that erupted over every perceived slight or transgression. While John was able to maintain a relationship with his own son, Chad, through a custody arrangement, he had no legal claim to Mitchell.

Mitchell finished high school and managed to receive a college degree, but never established any kind of meaningful career. Mitchell had been filching small amounts on jobs going all the way back to his earliest employment. Over the years he became bolder, stealing larger amounts and taking bigger chances. Although he was suspected on several occasions and outright fired from one job because of unverifiable suspicion, he was never prosecuted.

He also stole from family. He broke into our home and stole all of my silver, my family heirlooms. John was mortified and felt responsible. We pressed charges. When victim's services interviewed me and asked what I would like to have happen, I was willing to forgive Mitchell even though the silver was not retrievable. I said that I wanted Mitchell be in jail long enough to get sober, but that I wanted him to be placed in rehab after that because putting him in prison or jail long term would not be productive. As he had no prior convictions, they agreed and he received a short jail sentence followed by mandatory rehab. I learned later that he had also been stealing from his mother for many years although she had never reported it to the police.

Mitchell is 40 years old now. He expects to be taken care of by others, and yet he vocally claims his independence. He calls when he needs money; he feels that my husband owes this support to him because his childhood was messed up, that John should have rescued him somehow. At the same time, he will not accept any advice from us. He is unable to let go of the past and take responsibility for himself and his actions.

Over the years, Mitchell has had many emergency trips to the hospital because of his excessive drinking. I've lost count how many times he's landed in the hospital or rehab. We all rushed to the hospital again not long ago, certain that he was on his deathbed. He flat-lined as we hovered by his bedside. Thanks to heroic efforts by the ER team, they were able to revive him and he pulled through. After Mitchell was well enough to be released from the hospital, he went into rehab where he actually did quite well for a short time. Not long after his release, though, he fell back off the wagon. Without the constant support and structure of the rehab environment, he is unable to keep away from alcohol. He doesn't attend AA or other counseling services after he is discharged from rehab.

He's back in another facility now, trying to get sober. He places many obstacles between himself and sustainable sobriety, though. He has a hard time identifying with the people who are in there because, in his mind, he's smarter than they are. He does not try to connect with others. He doesn't acknowledge how his drinking has contributed to his deteriorating health. I don't believe he's ever dealt with the shame of breaking into my house and into his mother's house to steal. Even those things haven't been enough of a bottom for him to stay sober.

Mitchell didn't have a nurturing environment or caring adults in his formative years. He wasn't provided the support, guidance and basic sense of security that every child should receive. In the years that Mitchell has been a part of our lives, we've tried to give him a sense of family; of belonging and support. None of the trips to rehab seems to have made a positive impact. Yes, he had a rough start in life and carries scars from that, but he's well into adulthood and has been in charge of his own life for many years now. He has family who loves him and wants him to succeed, but he needs to take responsibility for his life, stop blaming others for his failures and his drinking, and be the man he could truly be.

He still drinks. He knows the risks. I don't know how many more chances he has left to turn his life around, because with Mitchell, another big hit and he's dead.

Our Thoughts

As well as this step-mother articulates the trajectory of Mitchell's life as an alcoholic, the contributing factors and likely outcome, both she and her husband John, Mitchell's step-father, do not seem prepared to withhold support, even knowing that rehab is only a temporary fix, a mere Band-Aid for a gaping wound. It's a tough call to withhold support when you know that a life is very possibly at stake if you don't underwrite another stay at rehab or hospital treatment.

Mitchell blatantly plays on John's sense of guilt for not having done more for him even though, legally, there was little he could have done to intercede on the boy's behalf. He's now a grown man who has been thrown repeated lifelines, welcomed into a family to which he has no blood ties, forgiven serious transgressions and provided second and third and fourth chances.

As long as a life hangs in the balance, our guess is that these stepparents will continue to come to the rescue, but Mitchell probably won't survive too many more "hits" as the story's narrator said. We hope that they provide support out of a sense of charity and not misplaced guilt. If, at some point, they decide to no longer bail him out, they need to prepare themselves to withstand Mitchell's efforts of manipulation, in whatever form they may come.

Celeste Weingardt & Irene Henry

DRY DRUNK
Jane's Story

This daughter stopped drinking several years ago, but as far as her mother can see, she hasn't changed anything else about her life, behavior or outlook.

Tara was the first grandchild on both sides of the family and was everyone's little princess. When she was three, I had another daughter; it was a huge shock to Tara when she wasn't the center of the universe anymore. A year later, I had a son who needed a lot of attention because of serious health problems, and that's really when Tara's behavior problems started: she would throw tantrums at home, in the grocery store, everywhere. My two other children were best friends beginning in their earliest years. Tara was their tormentor. It didn't help that my husband and I separated when they were all still in grade school. They lived with their father for several years after the divorce, then, one by one, came to live with me. It was really hard to be a mom and provide a home for the kids in the middle of trying to figure out my own life. We had plenty of fights and tears and hurt feelings.

By the time Tara was a teenager, her moods and angry rants were epic. She alienated just about everyone. She hooked up with a group of tattooed and pierced rebels who thought they were smarter than everyone else. I know that they were using drugs and drinking, but I really couldn't tell if Tara was into all that or not. My friends and I all liked to smoke a little pot and drink wine, so it didn't seem like a big deal that Tara did, too. She ended up in the alternative school program, not because she wasn't smart, but because she couldn't get along with others and was a nightmare for the teachers.

After high school she enrolled in an art school in San Francisco on her father's dime. It was such a relief when she moved out! Our relationship improved dramatically, but it was still easy for her to fly into a rage. Sometimes we would talk on the phone every week and sometimes she wouldn't speak to me at all for months at a time.

Tara met Tolek when she was 20, got pregnant, and ended up dropping out of school. They lived in the Tenderloin district, a part of San Francisco overrun by junkies and vagrants, the only area where they could afford the rent. They had a rocky relationship from the very start. Tolek drank a lot, and they fought – a lot.

One afternoon, Tara called, frantic, and begged me to come into the city to pick up Courtney, my granddaughter. When I got there, Tara was wasted. I hadn't ever seen her drunk before. She told me that I had to get her baby away from their place. I was a little freaked out. I may not have been the best mother in the world, but I was never falling down drunk or stoned around them. I packed a bag of clothes, diapers and a few stuffed animals for Courtney – Tara hadn't even managed to do that – and took my granddaughter home with me. Tara came to get her a couple of days later and seemed much better; sober and back in control of herself.

Later that year, she and Tolek moved closer to me, thinking that things would be easier out of the crowded, increasingly expensive city. The move didn't change much, though. Tara had trouble holding on to a job. After just a couple of months at a new job, she'd begin complaining about her boss, her co-workers, her hours and every other little thing. Sooner or later her mouth would get her fired. She couldn't just do her job and keep her thoughts to herself like the rest of us do. She still burned her way through relationships. She was always hot or cold, best friends or a mortal enemy, in constant contact or cutting off all communication. She and Tolek were always arguing. He started going to bars after work to avoid being at home with her, which just made her angrier.

When Courtney was two, I got another hysterical call from Tara while I was at work, demanding that I drop everything and come pick up my granddaughter immediately. She hung up before I was able to ask for details. I rushed over in a panic to find Tara fuming and blitzo drunk. Without any explanation or even a thank you to me for rushing over, she tore off to hunt down Tolek. She found him in a bar and they had a loud, ugly public fight. Someone called the cops and they both ended up being arrested. No surprise that they separated after that.

A couple of years after that, Tara told me that she was an alcoholic and had started going to AA. I don't think she's had a drink in nearly ten years now. To this day, she continues to go to the meetings, although I don't know what she gets out of them. She is still angry at the world. We had the most ridiculous argument over nothing at all important last year and she hasn't spoken to me since.

I have told her thousands of times over the years that I love her. I've apologized over and over, for whatever it was she feels I did wrong. I've told her that whatever I did wrong is in the past and that I am sorry for anything I did that hurt her, but can we just move forward now?

If I could go back in time, I would try to be closer to her. I wouldn't have left my husband in the way that I did. I think some of the anger comes out of that. But it is what it is. I don't know what else I can do or say. I miss her. I miss my granddaughter. It hurts not getting to see my granddaughter grow up.

I wish my daughter the best and hope for her sake that she finds happiness, but since I can't seem to help her, I can only do what is good for myself.

Our Thoughts

Tara is clearly the dominant personality in this relationship. Yes, the mom might have over-indulged Tara in her early years, which gave Tara a heightened sense of importance and a child's sense of betrayal when the spotlight shifted to include siblings, but the brother and sister came through this same situation OK after all.

This mother has, for years now, made amends to her daughter through both words and action. Tara's refusal to forgive her seems to us to be motivated by her desire to continue to control and dominate the relationship and to deflect blame for her own shortcomings.

Tara has attended AA meetings, but we agree with her mother that there is little evidence that she's getting much out of the program beyond not drinking, hence the title of this story, Dry Drunk, which refers to a person who does not drink but continues to behave in dysfunctional ways. There is no evidence of introspection or maturing. There was no mention that she's ever tried anger management or other counseling.

Mom recognizes that she hasn't been able to help Tara and that she needs to take care of herself. We hope that she can hold fast in her resolve to let go of the relationship and find peace in knowing that she has tried her best.

A Way Forward

Celeste Weingardt & Irene Henry

YOUR WELLBEING IS OUR PRIMARY CONCERN

We all wish the alcoholics in our lives could fix themselves. Wishes aside, we also know there is no sure-fire fix. And so we focus our intention in this writing on what you can do to minimize the impact of the drinker on you, the family member.

We focused on family because most of us are more willing to withstand the turmoil and try harder to salvage a relationship with a sibling, spouse, parent or child than we would with a person outside the immediate family. Of course there are exceptions. Family connections do not guarantee that special closeness, and there are certainly friends for whom we would go the extra mile.

We intentionally grouped the stories by familial relationship. A parent cannot speak to a spouse with a drinking problem in the same way she would approach her child, even an adult child. Family dynamics also color how one deals with a problem drinker.

Irene's multi-generational challenges with alcoholics (Like Father, Like Son) engendered markedly different responses to the alcoholics in her family, influenced by the specific aspects of each relationship. She cut off communication with the father who failed his family, but maintained contact with a brother who shared difficult years growing up despite his poor treatment of his siblings and mother.

Bob's desire to protect his stepdaughter (Hidden Bottles) outweighed his growing disdain for his wife. He stayed with her — even after her physical tirades, drunkenness and lying — in order to be a stabilizing presence in the household.

Perspective can get muddled, particularly when facing adverse situations. Not surprisingly, some of the people we interviewed had their self-identity challenged in dealing with the alcoholic in their family, an uncomfortable and confusing state.

Judy (Misplaying a Bad Hand) is an educated, former high school administrator who skillfully counseled students and parents navigate rough patches. She was adept in maintaining a professional distance while also showing compassion and empathy. Her self-image was that of an academic who could intellectualize her relationship with her brother, and yet she was continually challenged by her sense of responsibility as the older sibling, perhaps attempting to fill the role abandoned by their mother all those years ago.

Trisha (Waiting for the Inevitable) strived to live up to her understanding of Christian charity, a major tenet of her self-image, causing her years of grief beyond the time when she realized her efforts to help her sister were in vain. It wasn't until Trisha came to believe that her mother's safety was at stake that she was able to surrender to the reality that she cannot change her sister.

The collective image of Teresa's family (The Long Reach of Family) as being close knit was temporarily unraveled when they finally recognized their younger sister Barb had never felt included in the weave of the family fabric. Awareness led to openness and understanding, which enabled them to truly bring her into the family fold.

Regardless of why a person gets caught up in excessive drinking — genetic predisposition, self-medication, social anxiety, peer pressure, mental illness or any other reason — the result is the same. Alcohol takes control of their life.

Addiction, whether in the form of alcoholism, gambling, drugs, smoking or other manifestations, is a compulsion. It's something an alcoholic does against all logic, intellectual preference or recognition of how much they stand to lose.

Will power, self-awareness and self-esteem drown in a treacherous alcoholic brew. Some heavy imbibers may be able to hold their head above the turbulence for a long time, believing they are in control, unaware of the strong current that is pulling them ever closer to the falls. Some may ultimately welcome being swept away, too exhausted by the unrelenting force to keep trying. Others may recognize they are in trouble and try swimming for the bank. If they are lucky, they may have a friend or family member on shore holding out a line sturdy enough for them to grasp and be pulled to safety. It can be as scary for the friend on the bank as it is for the one who is in danger of drowning.

On Psychology Today's website (www.psychologytoday.com/basics/addiction), addiction is defined as "a condition that results when a person ingests a substance or engages in an activity that can be pleasurable but the continued use/act of which becomes compulsive and interferes with ordinary life responsibilities, such as work, relationships, or health. Users may not be aware that their behavior is out of control and causing problems for themselves and others."

Alcoholics Anonymous says, "Alcohol is cunning, baffling and powerful." We agree absolutely. It finds the small break in the dike and exploits it.

An after-work drink takes the hard edge off a tough day. A second extends the good vibe. Then drinking before dinner becomes routine. Why not a short one at lunch to see you through the afternoon crunch? Cunning.

The drinker starts making stupid mistakes at the office following a lunchtime glass or two. The six-pack after work ends with him snoring in front of TV every night, passed out. He vows not to drink during the day anymore and to limit himself to two beers in the evening. He's truly surprised to find himself drunk again the next night. Baffling.

His wife and he argue all the time now. She gives him an ultimatum: stop drinking or she's leaving. He loves her with all his heart. He would be lost without her. He goes a full month without drinking, then is handed a beer at a BBQ and the month of hard-earned sobriety evaporates like it never happened. Powerful.

For most alcoholics there is a propensity to add layers to their original problems, much like the way one lie leads to another until the situation is completely out of control. She might stop off at a bar instead of coming straight home after work, then lie about why she's late. She might hide bottles which will surely be discovered. Now she has to deal with broken trust, anger and resentment – all due to her drinking.

We have learned that drinking can be a reaction to or symptom of something else in the alcoholic's life. Depression. Social anxiety. Financial burdens. Poor health. Never having learned to cope with adversity because someone else always stepped in and took care of things. It isn't your responsibility to fix the drinker or their underlying problem, but once you identify likely contributing factors, you may be able to view their situation from a more holistic perspective and discover a previously hidden opportunity to have a positive influence.

NAVIGATING THE TRAPS

We humans have a great capacity to justify and rationalize our behavior. We can be extremely adept at rewriting our history and rearranging facts to suit our needs. A habitual drunk can look you straight in the eye and tell you any tale that will get him what he wants. He can twist his thinking around to such a degree that he comes to believe the lie himself, giving a false sheen of believability to his dishonest assertion.

The alcoholic's world is populated with mean bosses, thwarted opportunities and demanding wives. They are the victims and it is in your power to cut them a break. And if mere victimhood doesn't sway you, they'll lay on the guilt, as heavy as needed to get what they want.

Jo (Waiting for the Inevitable) would say whatever she needed you to believe in order to get you on her side. Even faced with a truth-revealing blood test, Jo continued to lie about being drunk. She burned through friendships. She manipulated people to make them feel sorry for her and give her money, booze or a place to crash. And when they stopped being her lackey, she'd discard them without a second thought.

Tara (Dry Drunk) discovered early in life that she could exert power over her mother through guilt. Tara accuses her mother of scarring her deeply by leaving her and her siblings (never mind that they both turned out fine) with their father when the parents divorced. She claimed that abandonment was the source of all of her problems, from drinking to anger issues. She perpetuated the blame through extended periods of non-communication, a painful and constant reminder to her mother that she damaged her daughter. As long as her mother bought into this narrative, Tara continued to hold it over her and avoided taking responsibility for her own circumstances.

Betty (The Illusion of a Privileged Life) explained away her need to drink as necessary to ease the anxiety caused by her husband's high-risk hobbies. Who could fault her for having an extra cocktail or two to calm her nerves when her husband was out flying planes or riding motorcycles all the time? She also excused her drinking on the fact that Doc frequently traveled for business, leaving her at home and lonely. In her mind, if only he'd been a little less self-involved and paid a bit of attention to her needs, she wouldn't have needed to drink.

Often out of work or under-employed, Larry (Prayers & Best Intentions), a prodigious manipulator, came to his sisters for money many times. And they rarely turned him down — even when they were fairly confident that it was within his means to manage his affairs on his own. Over the years, Larry was also a victim of other people's manipulation. He entered into several business relationships in which he was exploited. His self-esteem was degraded with each instance.

Mitchell (Lost at 40) took advantage of his stepfather's feelings of guilt for having left him with a mother whom he knew to be neglectful and capitalized on that leverage for years. His stepfather's current wife was also in the guilt by extension, to the point that she argued against Mitchell's incarceration after he stole valuable family antiques. These good people maintained their sense of culpability out of habit.

Guilt can be self-inflicted, too. Gail (The Illusion of a Privileged Life) was haunted by certainty that she contributed to her mother's drinking problem because she had been rebellious and difficult as a teen. She regretted not having made more of an effort to be closer to her mother in later years. Whether this sense of guilt was placed on Gail by her parents or was wholly self-induced, it is still misplaced. At some point every adult needs to take responsibility for their own life and wellbeing regardless of how others treat them.

Family members have a powerful hold on one another, making it that much more painful when we are betrayed by one of our own than it is to be duped or used by someone outside of the family. Throughout the individual stories in this book, we saw a constant stream of betrayal.

Jake (A Selfish Man) cheated on his wife over the course of their marriage. He freely dipped into their small budget to drink and carouse with one woman after another while his wife stayed home, caring for their children, worrying where he was and whether he'd come home that night.

Ben (Misplaying a Bad Hand) didn't have other women; his affair was with the bottle, choosing its company over his wife's night after night. Both of his wives ultimately left him because of the neglect as much as his alcohol fueled demeaning and berating treatment of them.

One could feel Irene's hot anger and pain in her narrative (Like Father, Like Son) about her father abandoning the family when she was a child although it happened decades ago. When a sibling flakes out it is hurtful. When a parent leaves, it is a traumatic event that can overshadow the rest of the child's development.

Mitchell (Lost at 40) stole from both his mother and from his stepfather's family. For him, as well as many other alcoholics and addicts, theft doesn't seem to register as a crime when it involves family. They help themselves to the contents of family member's wallets or sellable belongs whenever they have a need of a little extra cash.

We are all in favor of second chances, but if someone repeatedly betrays you, don't expect them to miraculously act differently without some exceptionally motivating incident forcing them to change their ways.

※

Intelligence is not necessarily an accurate indicator of how well we understand ourselves. One of humankind's strongest defense mechanisms is simply to deny that a problem exists. An alcoholic can be strongly motivated to discount his addiction, not wanting to deny himself something that brings him pleasure or comfort.

Tom (Drinking Buddies), a highly intelligent, accomplished lawyer is remains tight friends with his long times buddies, men who work hard running businesses and unwind with the same level of zeal that they employ in their careers. Tom is their equal by all measures except in his ability to curtail his drinking. He's quit drinking many times, sometimes for months or years, but time and again decides that he can drink casually, contrary to all evidence.

Ben (Misplaying a Bad Hand) takes the fact that he can go a couple of days (in isolated circumstances) without drinking as proof that he isn't an alcoholic. He digs in deeper each time someone challenges his drinking. When Ben's daughter cut a visit short because of his alcohol-fueled behavior, he convinced himself that the real reason she told him to leave was because her husband was trying to turn her against him. And when Judy presented the findings of her research into family genome markers, factors that make both of them high risk for alcoholism, Ben dismissed the information as completely without relevance to him.

Denial isn't the sole purview of the alcoholic. Loren's parents (Gone to Soon) were unable to accept the fact of their son's alcoholism. Even the doctor's diagnosis of liver damage caused by hard drinking was not enough to persuade Loren's mom.

To Arturo's daughter (The Patriarch), her father was simply a product of his culture. In this semi-rural, Mexican community it was socially acceptable for her father to go out drinking after a hard day's work, and to expect his laundry done, the house clean and dinner on the table when he got home. To question his drinking and his sexist treatment of her mother would have led to uncomfortable doubts about the substance and character of the man she had adored her whole life.

Denial can be a coping mechanism for anyone, alcoholic or not. It is one of the defensive walls we erect to protect us from truths or emotions we feel unable to face. So, sure, call them out on their denial. Tell them that they are only fooling themselves. Present them with examples. Possibly (one can always hope!) it will encourage newfound introspection.

All relationships are a balancing act of give and take. In a loving relationship, harmless indulgences bring us closer together. We make frequent compromises to move ahead with decisions. We argue to clear the air. These are all healthy and normal behaviors. Enabling, creating an environment of accommodation for an undesirable activity or action, even when motivated by love, is destructive and can throw a relationship out of balance.

As Boots (Boots) grew older, she evolved into an angry, difficult person to be around. She was marginally more pleasant when she was drinking and both Pat's father and brother indulged her drinking in order to calm the waters at home. Their enabling negated the impact of Pat's attempts to encourage his mother to stop drinking. Why should she listen to him when the others were supplying her with the beer she wanted? Since she did not drive, Boots would not have had a source of alcohol if family members hadn't provided it. Who knows how differently her life may have turned out if she had been forced to get along without her beer?

Jake (A Selfish Man) was an overbearing, aggressively dominating husband who bullied his wife, Diana. Although she was able to assert control over the running of the preschool, their home was Jake's castle and everyone tiptoed around his needs and moods. If he wanted to sit in front of the TV and drink a six-pack or spend his evenings out, it was always his choice and Diana nearly always let it go so as not to provoke him.

It's easy to fall into a pattern of enabling. We can be manipulated into it. We can do things against our better judgment out of guilt or love. We can do it because it's the easier short-term option. As in all things, awareness is the first step in fixing a problem.

Most of us can point to a handful of pivotal moments in our life that had a significant influence on our character, our way of interacting with the world or our path forward. Those key moments can be either good or bad. Not all traumatic experiences are of equal weight or continue to reverberate after the initial crisis has passed. Some traumas are the product of a single moment; some are the cumulative effect of a series of interconnected events. Whatever the cause of trauma, alcohol is one way to numb the pain.

Imagine how Ben (Misplaying a Bad Hand), a 14-year old boy, felt as he stood helplessly on the roadside witnessing his little sister first struck and then dragged to death by a passing automobile. And then layer that horror with the immense burden of guilt thrust upon him by his mother who lashed out at him in her grief, blaming him for his little sister's death. Other factors no doubt contributed to Ben's dependency on alcohol, but his sister firmly believed the accident, compounded by the mother's accusations, factored heavily in Ben's alcoholism.

Larry's (Prayers and Best Intentions) injury, losing vision in one eye (Prayers and Best Intentions), might seem far less a tragedy in comparison, but it noticeably altered his personality. He went through a depression following the accident that seemed to deflate him. Before the accident, he had been upbeat and optimistic about his future. Afterwards, he seemed resigned to a lesser life.

※

We do not profess to be mental health or addiction experts. We do know that, in many of the stories we heard, individuals who became addicted to alcohol also had mental health issues.

Diana (A Selfish Man) disregarded the early signs of Jake's mental illness as mere idiosyncrasies in spite of friends raising concerns about what they saw as erratic behavior. It was easy for her to assume that his bellicose behavior and frequent arguments was simply Jake passionately standing up for his politics. Diana romanticized his moodiness as part of his non-conformist persona. Plus, there were also days when he was upbeat and happy and life was fun and full of joy. When Jake began drinking, it was limited to a casual beer at first, but his consumption escalated, as did his unpredictable moods. His heavy drinking continued after he was officially diagnosed with manic depression. He resisted taking medications for his illness and refused what little counseling that was offered. It is possible his drinking was a form of self-medication as his symptoms became more pronounced.

Jo's (Waiting for the Inevitable) mental illness may have amplified or made it more difficult to tackle problematic behavioral patterns. From an early age she acted in ways that were both self-centered and self-destructive. She chose abusive partners. She abused drugs and alcohol. She repeatedly and intentionally hurt her sister, Trisha. Jo was professionally treated for both alcoholism and bipolar disorder with little improvement on either front.

There is no evidence that Sheila's second husband (Hidden Bottles) consulted an actual doctor or psychiatrist when he started medicating her with lithium for Bipolar Disorder. Sheila certainly had a trigger temper at times, but she also exhibited control over her outbursts when she recognized that it was in her best interest to do so. Not at all in keeping with the clinical symptoms of the illness. Her third husband, Bob, wisely discounted the amateur diagnosis. Sheila's behavior was challenging as well as baffling to him, though: hiding her bottles even though it was obvious that she drank, the fits of anger, the physical and verbal abuse. Yes, unacceptable, even outrageous behavior, but (probably) not mental illness. Sometimes people just aren't very nice.

Celeste Weingardt & Irene Henry

WHAT SUCCESS STORIES HAVE IN COMMON

Experts agree that a person will only stop drinking if they make that decision for themselves, but their road to recovery can be less fraught with ruts and wrong turns if they have a support system to help them along. The alcoholics profiled in our stories dealt with their alcoholism in vastly different ways. Nowhere was this more evident that when we parsed these narratives for examples of reaching out or trying to connect with others. Some were desperate to create, mend or hold on to connections. Others made little visible attempt.

Barb (The Long Reach of Family) finally found a supportive relationship with her fourth husband who attended AA meetings with her in her early days of sobriety. Together, they also became involved in charity work through the local church. Once Barb was able to share the trauma of her rape in high school and her feelings of alienation from her siblings, she and her sisters and brothers were able to work through the years of hurt and estrangement.

Alcoholic's Anonymous was a key component to Celeste's long-term sobriety (Prayers and Best Intentions). While she didn't formally complete the 12 steps, she gained insight into her behavior, learned to recognize her drinking triggers and acquired coping skills. Her husband took on a larger share of the parenting and household responsibilities so that she could attend as many as five AA meetings a week in the first year of recovery. As she developed new friendships and social skills, giving her the confidence to venture out into the larger community, her husband continued to be supportive and encouraging.

Connor (Making Good on Second Chances) also benefited from a supportive and understanding spouse. She stood by him in his darkest hour, willing to max out the credit card in order to give him the critical second

30-day stay in rehab. She continues to arrange the family schedule so that he can attend the 12-step meetings he needs. Connor's employer and co-workers have also been supportive and understanding in his recovery. He has found that staying close to the AA program and sponsoring other struggling alcoholics has been important to maintaining his own sobriety.

While AA played an important role in each of these recoveries, it is by no means a guarantee of sobriety – to which anyone familiar with the program will attest. And certainly, it is possible to break free of alcoholism without a formal 12-step program. Community involvement and an understanding and supportive family were also important components to their success. Celeste, Barb and Connor continue to be active in their communities. It is an ongoing journey.

Between the success stories and those who are still captive to alcohol are those who fall somewhere in between, achieving sobriety for long stretches but ultimately lapsing, destabilizing their future and damaging the trust of those closest to them. The cumulative toll on the family bonds caused by the intermittent drinking makes it difficult for family members to fully trust the alcoholic, which in turn creates a distance between them. It can become an irreparable chasm.

Larry (Prayers and Best Intentions) tried valiantly over the years to free himself from alcohol. Through much of his adult life he actively attempted to stay connected with family, with his church community, with Jesus. He sought out rehab programs. He made his way to homeless shelters. During long stretches of sobriety, he donated countless hours to volunteer efforts for the church. He joined Bible study classes and participated in counseling with the pastor. In his darkest hours, he summoned enough will to survive to make a call for help.

Tom (Drinking Buddies) continues to test his ability to drink casually, especially when friends with whom he has a long drinking history come to town. While he's been able to recover from each incident fairly quickly (so far), his wife's fears for their future together and her concern over the potential damage to the son who is also struggling to stay sober, all rise to the surface once again. At some point this two steps forward, one step back dynamic will become unsustainable.

The foundation of any enduring relationship is built on mutual trust. Love, family bonds cannot sustain without it. Lack of trust creates barriers: Can I really count on this person to have my back? To pick up our son on time? To tell me the truth?

Michael (Like Father, Like Son) regained the trust of his extended family by stepping up to care for his grandchildren when his daughter's lifestyle and circumstances rendered her unfit for the role. His sobriety, in fact, appeared to be primarily motivated by his determination to care for the grandchildren, making indirect amends perhaps, for the poor fathering he displayed with his own children. He showed himself to be capable and reliable and up to the challenge of raising these children.

After Barb (The Long Reach of Family) started on her road to recovery and opened up to her siblings, her sisters were quick to embrace her back into the fold. But it took a while for her to gain the trust of some of her brothers. She had to prove herself over an extended period of time by staying sober, taking ownership of the angst she caused within the family and being generally reliable.

As much as Janet (Making Good on Second Chances) wanted to trust and support her husband, she was never been able to completely drop her guard when it came to Connor's sobriety. He lied to her before about quitting, and she missed all the signs — how could she be sure she wasn't missing them again? Connor was sensitive to her ongoing concerns and worked hard to allay her fears, staying active in AA, being involved in family life and having candid conversations with her, even when it was uncomfortable.

Sometimes love means taking a leap of faith, but these family members also wisely required a track record of accountability in order to rebuild trust.

Role models can be intentional or accidental. They can model positive actions and outlooks or bad. A person is never too old to benefit from the wisdom and experience of others. A mentor can be specifically asked to fill that role, or it can be someone unaware that they are serving that function.

The program of Alcoholic's Anonymous is successful for many who want to get sober in large part because of their group support as well as one-on-one sponsorships where individuals who have spent time in the program and turned their own life around serve as an advisor and personalized support system for newcomers. Sometimes it is a short-term relationship. For others, like Connor (Making Good on Second Chances), it is a continuing commitment. He's now been a part of AA for a number of years and is himself a sponsor to others, newer to the program than he. These constant conversations about their shared experiences, their battles with drinking, help to re-enforce his personal vigilance against the temptation to drink again.

Once Celeste (Prayers and Best Intentions) opened herself up to the possibility of connecting with others, friendly people entered her life. Through those connections, she discovered previously unimagined opportunities to get involved in issues she cared about, but had never known how. Feeling less accomplished and intimidated by the people she was meeting, she embraced the cliché, "to act as if, and the rest will follow". She identified several women who she privately chose to be her role models and mentors, observing how they interacted with others, how they came to meetings prepared, listened to others, were respectful and respected. Years later, she confided to one of these women how she had served as a role model, who was delighted to have, however unwittingly, been helpful.

We are all mentors and role models to someone. Pay attention to what it is about your own role models that draws you to them. Look at how you interact with the world and give some thought to how your actions will be viewed and emulated by those who look up to you.

TAKING CONTROL

Through the stories we have shared, you have heard from some who have regrets for not having done more and others who resented the burden of their perceived responsibility to care for, prop up or otherwise accommodate the alcoholic. This is an immensely emotionally charged personal decision to be made based on a multitude of factors. Ask yourself: How is this alcoholic affecting my life and wellbeing? What changes are within my control? How will my choices impact my relationship with other family members? Am I prepared to let go?

Each of us has our own line in the sand, a point at which we will walk away. For us, that meant knowing that we did all we could and let go when we saw that our efforts were to no avail. We do not want to be haunted by thoughts that we could have done more; conversely, we cannot allow ourselves to be consumed by someone else's alcoholism, however much we may love them.

In several narratives, family members consciously and actively set boundaries with the alcoholic in their life.

Ben's sisters (Misplaying a Bad Hand) decided to only initiate contact with Ben in the morning hours, before he starts drinking for the day, knowing that he became increasingly combative in direct proportion with the amount of beer consumed. If he called them in the afternoon or evening, they chose to be as unresponsive as possible, recognizing the futility in correcting or challenging his opinions in any way.

Janet (Making Good on Second Chances) attached a non-negotiable condition to her support when Connor went into rehab. She would stand by him and aid him in any way she could while he worked on his recovery, but she made it absolutely clear that she would not tolerate another relapse. She had been devastated by his deceit as much as his drinking and was not willing to put herself through that kind of anguish and turmoil again.

Tom's wife (Drinking Buddies) was terrified at the thought that he would have the kids in the car with him while he was driving under the influence. For some time after the incident when their son called her, scared to get into the car with Dad because he was so obviously drunk, she was adamant that Tom not drive the children anywhere until she felt that he could be trusted again.

Regardless of whether the perimeters in these examples were set in an effort to change the behavior of the alcoholic, protect other family members or purely for self-preservation, the boundaries were narrowly defined and a continuing relationship could exist as long as the boundaries were respected.

*

Not all relationships are salvageable. Too often the alcoholic's sphere of destruction reaches a point where loved ones feel they have no other option than to stop trying to save a relationship that is beyond repair. That doesn't mean they necessarily stop loving or caring about the person. It means that they can no longer tolerate the pain, frustration, disappointment and anger that overwhelm the relationship.

Kim's life (I Choose) had been in upheaval for years. She knew that the root cause was the dysfunctional relationship she had with her alcoholic husband. Her 'aha' moment was realizing she could make a choice about how she moved forward. Ending a relationship with someone she had planned to spend the rest of her life with was heart wrenching, but once the decision was made, a suffocating dark cloud was lifted from her and she could see the sun rising on the horizon for the first time in a long while.

Trisha (Waiting for the Inevitable) finally made the hard choice to end all contact with Jo when she began to fear that Jo might physically harm her mother. She was also motivated by her feelings of intense guilt for having exposed her children and husband to the fallout of Jo's toxic actions for so many years. When Trisha accepted the reality that Jo's treatment of others over the years has gotten worse in spite of her attempts to help, she was able to focus instead on what was within her power to protect herself and the rest of her family. Today, she is resigned to her belief that Jo will never get better, but also relieved that she no longer has to deal with the constant strain Jo created in her life.

For Irene (Like Father, Like Son) the letting go process with her father, Roger, was not a conscious effort. He had been abusive drunk, terrorizing the family as far back as she could remember. When he left, she felt relief more than anger. And when he attempted to reconcile some years later, she had no need for him in her life. She had learned to value loyalty and kindness, both attributes lacking in his character – with or without alcohol.

After years of trying to mend the relationship with her daughter, Jane (Dry Drunk) has reluctantly called it quits. She can't harden her heart and stop caring about her daughter's wellbeing entirely, but can give herself permission to create a buffer of emotional distance for her own peace, if not exactly happiness. She feels that she has given it her best effort and now it's up to Tara to initiate any future reconciliation.

What does letting go mean for you? Can you create sufficient emotional distance simply by acknowledging that the alcoholic's problems are not your responsibility and tolerate being in their presence at family functions? Will you have to completely sever all contact to be free of the burden that the alcoholic's proximity imposes on you? What will it take to get your own life back on track?

Most of us mere mortals resist making monumental changes unless forced to do so. By reading about how others grappled with the decision to let go, we hope that you will be better prepared to face your own dilemma.

FINAL THOUGHTS

Even after all the interviews, conversations and research that went into writing this book, we remain unsure about why some individuals succumb to alcoholism while others who seemingly face greater adversity do not. Our approach and our advice to you are to view each alcoholic as the unique and complex individual that they are and deal with them accordingly.

The level of time, effort and compassion that you are willing to expend in maintaining a relationship with the alcoholic in your life is influenced by many factors. Whether you are reading this book because you want to salvage your relationship or are at your wits end and are trying to figure out how to cut this person out of your life, make your decisions deliberately and with forethought rather than reactively. Figure out what is best for you and make that your guiding light.

- Be aware of the red flags that we have identified and look for others.
- Be deliberate in your choices to engage with or lend assistance to the alcoholic.
- Set boundaries.
- Don't allow the alcoholic to take you down with them.
- Be kind to yourself.
- Your feelings are valid.
- Don't live in regret.
- Write your story. Whether you share it with others or not, just the act of pouring your thoughts and feelings onto the page can be cathartic. It was for us.

If you glean ideas from this book that will help you assist the alcoholic in your life to put down the bottle for good, that would be awesome, but we know too well that sobriety is ultimately up to the alcoholic themselves, regardless of how great the support they receive from family, friends or professionals.

RESOURCES

The following is a short list of resources that will enhance your understanding of the dynamics between yourself and the alcoholic in your life. Several offer valuable tips on how to assert control over the relationship.

Enabling

www.psychologytoday.com/blog/the-anatomy-addiction/201207/are-you-empowering-or-enabling
https://psychcentral.com/lib/are-you-an-enabler/
http://www.hazeldenbettyford.org/articles/kala/enabling-fact-sheet

Saying No

https://psychcentral.com/lib/learning-to-say-no/
https://tinybuddha.com/blog/stop-saying-yes-want-say-no/

Coping

https://addictionresource.com/alcohol-rehab/alcoholism/living-with-an-alcoholic/
https://www.verywell.com/things-to-stop-if-you-love-an-alcoholic-67300

Support Groups

http://www.adultchildren.org/
https://al-anon.org/

There are many factors that can play a role in whether a person becomes an alcoholic. Heredity. Environment. Culture. DNA. Trauma. There are smart folks in science, medicine, religion, psychology, anthropology and other fields of study exploring these influences. Researchers are currently looking into a connection between addiction and an enzyme that degrades dopamine. Someday, perhaps in our lifetime, there may be breakthroughs in treatment as simple as a daily pill to hold alcoholism in check.

Here are links to get you started if you wish to do some independent research.

Alcoholism: Causes and Treatment
Alcohol MD
www.alcoholmd.com/causesofalcoholism.htm
www.alcoholmd.com/typesofalcoholism.htm
National Institute on Alcohol Abuse and Alcoholism Facts and Statistics
www.niaaa.nih.gov/alcohol-health/overview-alcohol-consumption/alcohol-facts-and-statistics
Gene mutation linked to excessive alcohol drinking
www.sciencedaily.com/releases/2013/11/131126123931.htm
Childhood conduct disorder
www.nature.com/mp/journal/v9/n1/full/4001368a.html
Dopamine and Substance Abuse
http://onlinelibrary.wiley.com/doi/10.1111/gbb.12147/abstract
New Approaches in Treating Addiction as a Disease
www.psmag.com/health-and-behavior/five-studies-treating-addiction-as-disease
The Genetics of Alcohol and Other Drug Dependence
http://pubs.niaaa.nih.gov/publications/arh312/111-118.pdf

No recommendation or guarantee of services or facts related to these resources is implied by the authors.

Celeste Weingardt & Irene Henry

ACKNOWLEDGEMENTS

Our everlasting gratitude to Mary, Teresa, Judy, Trisha, Diana, Kimberly, Janet, Bob, Pat, Irma, Gail, and to the others who wish to remain anonymous, for sharing their stories with us. We could not have written this book without each of them taking a leap of faith in trusting us to honor their story in the retelling. We greatly appreciate their openness and candor in reliving the distressing memories of intimate family relationships.

Thanks to Judy Bysshe, Sharon Hillbrant and Victoria Bortolussi for reading our mess of a first draft and providing candid and helpful critiques.

Thanks to Colleen Kimmett (https://reedsy.com/colleen-kimmett) for her terrific editing. Colleen's patience and tact in gently encouraging us to cut, rephrase and generally clean up our writing was invaluable.

Thanks also to Allison Gibson for her encouragement and generosity in sharing her wealth of knowledge in writing and publishing; to The Binders, a social media community for women writers, through which we connected with our editor; to Carina Armenta for spot-on suggestions of final tweaks; to Roger Thompson, author of My Best Friend's Funeral, for letting us pick his brains about publishing and book promotion; to the Ventura County chapter of Small Publishers, Artists & Writers Network (SPAWN) and the Independent Writers of Southern California (IWSC) and for their informative and immensely helpful workshops.

ABOUT THE AUTHOR

Celeste Weingardt

Celeste began writing about her brother following his death, in an effort to better comprehend how alcohol influenced the trajectory of his life. Recognizing that many people struggle to understand loved ones in the grip of alcoholism, the writing project evolved to include the personal accounts of others. Her hope in sharing these stories is that it will provide clarity and direction to people in similar circumstances.

Irene Henry

Irene Henry, one of four children, was raised in Illinois. She is a law school graduate, political activist, insurance agent, former high school volleyball coach and mom of two. She has shared experiences with alcoholism both personally and professionally. Irene resides in California with her very patient husband.

author@inthedrink.info
https://tinyurl.com/inthedrinkbook

Made in the USA
San Bernardino, CA
24 March 2019